W9-CAV-186

THE

MANAGERIAL

MIND

THE

MANAGERIAL

MIND

David W. Ewing

THE FREE PRESS, *New York*

COLLIER-MACMILLAN LIMITED, *London*

Copyright © 1964 by The Free Press of Glencoe
A DIVISION OF THE MACMILLAN COMPANY

Printed in the United States of America

All rights reserved. No part of this book may be reproduced or transmitted in any form or by any means, electronic or mechanical, including photocopying, recording, or by any information storage and retrieval system, without permission in writing from the Publisher.

Collier-Macmillan Canada, Ltd., Toronto, Ontario

Library of Congress Catalog Card Number: 64-16957

First Free Press paperback edition 1968

ACKNOWLEDGMENTS

THE IDEA AND TITLE for this book were suggested by an article by Charles E. Summer, Jr., in the *Harvard Business Review* (January-February, 1959).

At many points I have used concepts set forth in sermons by Duncan E. Littlefair, minister of the Fountain Street Baptist Church in Grand Rapids, Michigan, as a springboard for my own thinking.

The short excerpts from cases copyrighted by the President and Fellows of Harvard College are reprinted by permission. Such cases are not necessarily intended to illustrate either correct or incorrect, desirable or undesirable management policies or procedures.

For helpful criticisms and suggestions I am indebted to Edward C. Bursk and, at early stages in the manuscript, to Ordway Tead and Richard B. McAdoo.

The manuscript was prepared for the publisher by Miss Diana Lees.

A great deal of help came from my wife throughout the writing period.

D. W. E.

CONTENTS

INTRODUCTION

MANY PEOPLE TODAY seek a better understanding of the managerial mind. They are curious about the special attitudes, if any, that a manager brings to his work. They wonder about the assumptions he makes and the values he develops, and they are especially interested in sizing up these attitudes and values. Do they form a consistent pattern? Are they stimulating? What effects do they have?

The manager is a fixture in many fields—business, government, education, the military, professional organizations, and others. He is the boss, the man who gets results not by his own hand but through the efforts of others. He supervises, he directs, he co-ordinates the activities of employees reporting to him. Not surprisingly, he is not the easiest man in an organization to identify with. But while as a person he may be hard to understand, his position is always sought for the money, power, and prestige that go with it. Always, too, the position seems to have an effect on the mind of the man in it—not only a moral and ethical effect (which is the aspect novelists and playwrights usually discuss), but also an influence on his way of approaching a problem or situation (which is the aspect with which this book is concerned). Often this influence is great enough so that a manager consciously looks for successors who show a special capacity to be influenced in the same way he thinks he was influenced. When this happens, an ever-strengthening cycle develops in which the effect of managers on managerial positions is reinforced by the effects of the positions on the managers, and *vice versa*.

Interest in the managerial mind is increasing among an impressive variety of groups:

Engineers, scientists, and other technical specialists. The "research revolution" has made such men indispensable in business, government, and other fields. If at first there was a notion that they could be limited to purely technical assignments, that illusion has been completely dispelled. Borne into organizations on the tides of new technologies, many have been "beached" permanently in management positions because only they could supervise technical work with sufficient understanding. Many, too, have shown real capacity as managers. Yet, while they know they are needed in administration, they may be torn by doubts that it offers enough intellectual challenge. Can they earn the same high respect that they enjoyed as professional men?

Accountants, financial analysts, market researchers, and other staff men. These men have been brought closer and closer to top management by the "information revolution"—the increasingly crucial role of accurate "intelligence" quickly obtainable. In this process many have slipped into executive positions—as much by accident as by intent—while others are on the verge of crossing over. Both groups are inclined to wonder. They have been trained in areas where there were standards, patterns of thought, consistency, which were intellectually satisfying. Does administration offer similar satisfactions?

Lawyers, doctors, and other professional people. Some of these men have become administrators in order to direct the services of their own professions. Many law firms, for instance, are themselves growing businesses. Hospitals, clinics, and medical groups have become enterprises fully as important as those in commerce and industry. In both cases, management is necessary. One member of a law firm becomes a full- or part-time manager, although he is still called an attorney; a physician often spends more time supervising medical work than practicing medicine. Here again there can be no doubt of the necessity of what they are doing, but they cannot help comparing the new duties of supervision to the customary duties of professional practice. As lawyers and doctors, they had a special approach, a clear methodology. What does administration offer in that line?

Students. The student is less inclined today than ever before to choose a career simply because it is that of his father or his friends. He is exposed to many possibilities. Sometimes men come to his school or college and speak persuasively about the advantages of their own fields. He ponders. Should he try administration in preference to other fields? What about the suggestion from a writer or teacher that managerial life by nature tends to be self-seeking, power-grubbing, and "dog-eat-dog"?

Administrators. Career administrators are themselves interested in probing the managerial mind. They do not need to be told that enormous advances have been made in the twentieth century both in knowledge and in training for management. But what about the mind of the manager himself? What attitudes and assumptions underlie his use of knowledge?

It is very important to realize that the questions these groups ask and the needs they express are not satisfied by simple facts about the importance, prestige, power, or money that goes with a good managerial post. Nor does it suffice to describe the wealth of useful knowledge now available on methods and policies, vital as that knowledge may be. What all these men want to know is the pattern of values, standards, and assumptions that makes a thoughtful administrator's thinking different from that of other people.

Without such an understanding, we tend to be cynical about the managerial mind. If we are already in management work, we may downgrade it, or we may feel a kind of inferiority complex about what we are doing. If we are not yet in management, we may have to justify going into it on such grounds as "My family needs the money" or "Somebody has to do it—why not me?" Lest there be any doubt that these feelings are real among various types of people in business, government, and research, let me offer a few examples.

"To run a company, I think, takes a good second-class mind," the head of an enterprising small firm told a business school case-writer. "If you have a first-class mind, you go mad. . . . " I myself have run into the same type of reaction many times—in talks with businessmen and in the manuscripts they write. Sometimes, in fact, it seems to me that this reaction colors one's whole attitude toward business. After the Thirtieth Annual Business Conference at the Harvard Business School, Dean Stanley F. Teele reported: "At least three times during the conference, I had a man say to me, in differing words but in essence, 'I wonder whether there would be any possibility of my shifting from business to teaching. Before I am through, I should like to do something really socially useful.' " [1]

"You can't think and be in government at the same time," a federal administrator explained to a reporter. He too has plenty of company—good men in important government positions who are not *conscious,* at least, that they too have a special mode of thinking as do the lawyer, doctor, scientist, and engineer. In fact, I think they do. Almost everything they read, however, suggests that the qualities required are common sense, courage, determination, sense of mission, and so forth—qualities that good men in almost any important calling would be expected to need.

The research director of one large firm was a chemist, the holder of many patents in use, as well as a sensitive, persuasive, highly respected manager. He was discussing with some other men the problem of getting research personnel to put the company's interests first in their work. While noting that young physicists and other scientists were not likely to do so, he observed that nevertheless they were the *real* scientific resources of the company. But, he was asked, wasn't he a scientist? Why did he exempt himself? "He

---

1. Dan H. Fenn, Jr., ed., *Managing America's Economic Explosion* (New York: McGraw-Hill Book Company, Inc., 1961), p. 266.

said, 'Hell, I'm not a scientist now. I don't spend the time I used to spend in the lab. It's true that I've picked up a good deal of this and that in my time. I throw a good idea into the hopper now and then, but I'm not the one who works it through.' Questioned as to whether this were not an important contribution, he said, 'Yes, it's a supplement to scientific activity.' Later in the conversation he used the term 'ancillary' to refer to similar activity. *It was pointed out that he referred to what he did* [*i.e., management*] *in terms which suggest the second-rate, the nice-to-do, but not really significant. He said, 'I guess I feel that way.'* " [2]

Here again, obviously, the manager did not associate administrative thinking with a strong pattern of values and attitudes similar to those of scientists and other professional men, or, if he did, he did not consider that pattern significant and satisfying.

The aim of this book is to identify for the manager and the prospective manager certain values and attitudes that distinguish the administrator from men in other callings, vocations, and professions. The emphasis will be on the things that set the administrator apart, that make his approach different, that make his contribution significant. In many respects, surely, his mind must be like any other good mind. We are interested here not so much in its similarities as in its dissimilarities.

This book is one of reflections, not of research findings. It is an attempt to interpret the way administrators think, with no claim that that way is necessarily the best one or that it always characterizes managerial actions. It is important to note that this mode of thought is an evolving one, not yet fully crystallized. Indeed, there have been only a few isolated attempts to define it at all, with most of the emphasis being placed instead on such concepts of administration as organization or control, executive techniques, or personality patterns. It is timely, then, to try to identify the managerial mind now, for the ideas we set forth— the images we raise—can perhaps help administrators to articulate and discuss what they believe in, so that their habits of thought will find quicker acceptance.

---

2. David B. Gleicher, "Choice, Status, and Self-Esteem in Science" (Cambridge: Arthur D. Little, Inc., 1962), pp. 3-4. The italics are mine.

Most of the material from which I have drawn comes from a business setting, but enough of it involves managers in government, education, and the military to suggest that the attitudes described apply in organizations across the board. The most important part of the material consists of cases on administration, histories of organizations, and biographies.

In case it is not clear from the context, let me emphasize here that this volume is *not* about personality traits but about values, points of view, and ideas; *not* about executives in general but only about those whose job is primarily to supervise the work of others. A brief summary of the major points is included in the last chapter.

THE

MANAGERIAL

MIND

1

THE

MANAGERIAL

EMPHASIS:

COMMITMENT TO

THE ORGANIZATION

IF THERE IS A MANAGERIAL MIND, there must be some central feature that distinguishes it from other "minds." For example, the distinguishing feature of the legal mind may be an ideal of justice, which leads to the presumption of innocence, reliance on precedent, rules of evidence, and other such principles. The key to the medical mind may be absorption with individual health, while the leading aspect of the scientist's thinking is the value placed on knowledge and the preoccupation of the trader is with profit.

What makes the approach of the administrator fundamentally different from the approaches of men and women in other vocations? Is the difference that his values are a kind of composite of other groups' values—a unique blend—or is his thinking distinguished by a new ingredient?

The idea of a composite is appealing and, up to a point, plausible. There can be no question, for instance, that thoughtful administrators are concerned with such ideals as justice, individual welfare, knowledge, and efficiency—or with such goals as profit and power. The trouble is that these concerns are not dominant or consistent enough in any combination to make a convincing pattern of motivation. We find too many of what the statistician might call "random variations" in the record. Sometimes the administrator attaches a high premium to justice, individual welfare, or efficiency—but sometimes he does not. And the times when he does not may be crucial ones that cannot easily be explained away. Furthermore, sometimes his actions flatly contradict his professed ideals. The person seeking consistent logic in the manager's actions, using conventional criteria, may well throw up his hands in despair. At the moment he becomes convinced that one combination of ideas is the key, the manager makes a vital decision that contradicts it—and is meant to do so.

Occasionally we try to account for such aberrations by calling them exceptions to a rule. The manager is usually motivated by humanitarian goals, we explain, but at times he must sacrifice them to be practical. Or we argue that the manager's ultimate goal is public service, but he must make short-run compromises.

Is there not, however, some central theme in the administrative point of view to which there are no important exceptions? I think there is. First, however, we must start afresh. Borrowed concepts of what is important won't do; we must go at the problem inductively. Various kinds of information from primary sources are helpful. We can examine actual cases of administrative experience, documents of certain episodes, as well as histories and biographies. We can consider articles that managers write for professional journals, preferably those pieces that reflect a good deal of soul-searching. We can talk with managers and watch them work. If we analyze all of these sources, one thing stands out: *The most important feature of the managerial mind is its commitment to the life and growth of the organization.* Whether the organization is an assembly room in a manufacturing plant, a government bureau, a college, a military unit, or a large corporation with far-flung divisions, the aim of the administrator is to keep it operating and thriving. To him this objective has the same central importance as health to the physician, profit to the speculator, knowledge to the researcher.

Significantly, this dedication to the organization is revealed in an endless variety of ways—in pleas to do a better job of selling the organization's services to outsiders, in efforts to improve financial control, in attempts to perfect statistical techniques. In technologically advanced industries, it underlies the painstaking efforts of project managers to focus the attention of engineers and scientists on the project at hand rather than on the next job to which they may be assigned. There are many similar examples, some of them conflicting. For instance, both the man who delegates freely and the man who does not may be motivated by the same concern for their department or enterprise. Commitment to the organization is the lowest common denominator of their approaches; they differ in method, not principle.

Why is the organization considered so important? An obvious first reason is that it offers personal opportunities for advancement, prestige, security, contact with people, and other satisfactions.

Second, the organization is one of the chief instruments for accomplishment in modern society. In manufacturing, buying, publishing, counseling, education, rehabilitation and service, war, law enforcement, philanthropy—in these and many other activities people are finding it increasingly difficult to accomplish worthwhile objectives outside the organization.

Third, the manager values the organization because it provides jobs for people. He does not have to see the elation on the faces of many newly hired men or the worry and chagrin among those who have been laid off, to develop a strong emotional (as well as intellectual) commitment to the growth of his department or enterprise.

Fourth, many managers have come to value an organization because of family ties, friends, and other personal associations. It is significant that paternalism and nepotism are associated with some of the fiercest struggles for survival among business firms. To offer only one illustration, during the severe depression of 1857, the great bridge-builder John Roebling (responsible for the Niagara, Ohio, and Allegheny bridges, as well as the concept behind the Brooklyn Bridge) made heroic efforts to keep his wire and rope company going. Banks were closing everywhere, and factories were shutting down. Fearing that demand for his product might fall to practically nothing during the forthcoming year, he wrote to his superintendent at Trenton:

> You should go to Philadelphia and purchase . . . a lot of provisions, say $300 worth—flour, bacon, ham, coffee, sugar, molasses, rice, etc. for our own use, your household, and all the hands in our employment. Let all the hands understand that they will have to take one-half their wages in provisions & groceries & coal. You can convert the south part of the cellar of the new house into a store room. . . . This will not only be a saving all around, but also a great service to our hands. We may be able by this means to employ our good old hands all winter & make rope ahead, and also wire. Mr. Riedel & Washington can manage this store business, & keep a book of entries in the store room, to be squared up every week. . . . Perhaps it will be well to order an additional boatload of Stove Coal from the Schuylkill region (to be paid with Philadelphia money) for the use of our hands and our own.[1]

In short, Roebling saw himself as father to the firm, and he was as determined to preserve it and its employees as a father is determined to save his family under attack.

Fifth, it may seem important to preserve an enterprise simply because it is there. It has a presence, an identity, and instinct says to

---

1. D. B. Steinman, *The Builders of the Bridge* (New York: Harcourt, Brace and Company, 1945), p. 210.

keep it going. At a Harvard Business School conference, thirty businessmen were discussing "Debate at Wickersham Mills," a *Harvard Business Review* article describing different stockholders' feelings about what to do about the future of a certain textile firm. (The firm was fictional but based on an actual case.) In the article, one of the stockholders—Charles—argued in favor of selling out instead of trying to keep the company intact. Most of the businessmen in the discussion had an aversion to Charles's viewpoint. Abram T. Collier, author of the article and vice-president of an insurance company, commented on their feelings: "Is it fair to say that all of us who are tied up in organizations have a feeling of wanting that organization to survive, just as we want to survive as individuals? And to give up—to give up in the sense that Charles is doing—is to violate something that is one of the deepest feelings we have." [From the transcript of the discussion.] These managers might well agree with March and Simon that:

> Organizations are assemblages of interacting human beings and they are the largest assemblages in our society that have anything resembling a central coordinative system. Let us grant that these coordinative systems are not developed nearly to the extent of the central nervous system in higher biological organisms—that organizations are more earthworm than ape. Nevertheless, the high specificity of structure and coordination within organizations—as contrasted with the diffuse and variable relations *among* organizations and among unorganized individuals—marks off the individual organization as a sociological unit comparable in significance to the individual organism in biology.[2]

Unique Priority

The manager's sense of commitment to the organization means that he places a high priority on the processes of administering, supervising, and coordinating. He will worry more about them, interrupt his schedule to give them extra attention, or defer

---

2. James G. March and Herbert A. Simon, *Organization* (New York: John Wiley & Sons, Inc., 1958), p. 4.

other matters until he can attend first to the problem of how people work together. In a documentary study of change in a growing company, Paul R. Lawrence reports a meeting between a district manager of a supermarket chain and a group of store managers. The district manager tells them:

> Now I want to make it clear that [the new store manager] has a responsibility to me for running this store right, and each one of you as department heads have a responsibility to [him] to see that you are running your own department right. Now I want to make this perfectly clear (standing up) that I don't think you [cash department head] are always carrying out your responsibility on this kind of thing. For instance, if [my wife] walks up to check out her food, you are all bowing and scraping and doing everything you can to be pleasant and nice and helpful to her. Now that's all right, and you have a responsibility to the customer, but I am not sure you are thinking at that particular moment—is my chief responsibility to this customer or is it to see that the five or six other people that are working for me at the different cash registers are doing what they should be doing to give the customers the service we want to give them? But, if that other thing isn't being taken care of, that should take priority over your being nice to [my wife]. That is your responsibility. Of course you have to worry about the customer, but you must primarily worry about whether your men are looking out for the customer or not. I think that is something you've got to learn to do.[3]

In other words, the district manager is reminding the store managers that their first job is administration. He is telling them that, while the ultimate objective of their organizations is profit, immediate results are the business of clerks, not supervisors. This district manager would probably agree that no organization can survive for long unless it meets a real need. On the other hand, he might point out that needs cannot be met unless there are organizations ready to meet them. "I'm going to be interested in foremen who can develop good men for the company," an execu-

---

3. Paul R. Lawrence, *The Changing of Organizational Behavior Patterns: A Case Study of Decentralization* (Boston: Harvard Business School Division of Research, 1958), pp. 100-101.

tive at the Goodyear Tire & Rubber Company used to tell his supervisors. "Men are more important than goods." [4]

Note how different the managerial mind is in this respect from other minds. Take a design engineer, for instance. He is personally responsible for sketches, specifications, measurements, and so forth. His primary involvement is in creating a specific product. As a member of a firm or organization, he will do well *not* to worry much about other people's problems. Similarly, a political reformer may gladly exploit a particular government agency to accomplish a certain goal in antitrust policy or food inspection, even sacrificing the agency, if necessary, to accomplish the goal. To him the cause is the important thing, not the organization.

To the businessman whom we call a trader—a professional buyer and seller of companies, for example, the organization is important only as long as he has his money in it. It is a device to him, an elaborate cash register, and he has his eye on the day when he can count his chips and pull out with a handsome capital gain. The trader may contribute greatly to the economic growth of a region or industry; countless traders have done so. But he contributes only indirectly (if at all) to the cellular, organic, lifelike growth that characterizes a dynamic organization.

The professional administrator takes an aggressive interest in the unending series of problems and "troubles" that arise in organizational life. He regards the solution of such problems not as an extracurricular aspect of his job but as a central and significant focus of attention. "Theoretically a store manager has nothing to do," one food-chain executive has said. "Nevertheless, keeping everyone happy and maintaining our standards does in fact amount to a full-time job for him." [5] That is part of it—simply watching for problems, being on hand to help, revising where needed. How it is done is a matter of personal preference. Some

4. P. W. Litchfield, *Industrial Voyage* (New York: Doubleday & Company, Inc., 1954), p. 129.
5. Supreme Markets, Inc., a Harvard Business School case. Copyright by the President and Fellows of Harvard College.

men choose to set up efficient reporting systems and develop carefully supervised channels of communication. Others go to the opposite extreme and make a fetish of personal contact. For men in both groups, however, the motive is the same.

THE STRUGGLE AGAINST DISINTEGRATION

The administrator's commitment to his department or enterprise is sharpened by his fear of what will happen if he does not battle for its survival. He knows that an organization is continually subject to the strain of explosive, disintegrating forces. Personal animosities and jealousies, misunderstandings, conflicting interests—these forces and many others work against unity and cohesiveness. They may flare up at a moment's notice when things go wrong or when there is an absence of direction. They are always present, with the power to blow the structure of cooperation to bits should management weaken.

The United States Forest Service is a case in point. Over the years, devoted administrators have succeeded in building it into a strong and effective agency, but their victory over the tendencies toward fragmentation is never finally won. A close student of the Forest Service points out:

> The centrifugal tendencies . . . are not momentary phenomena, which, when counteracted, cease to operate. They are merely held in check by integrative forces greater than they, and every lapse of integrative power is promptly followed by symptoms of dissolution, as was the case, for instance, when the control of Forest Service policy slipped from Washington into the hands of the regional foresters. It takes constant effort to keep the members of a large organization responsive to leadership from the center.[6]

In this agency, as in countless others, members obviously are swayed by many influences other than commitment to the organization. The Rangers come to their jobs with differing customs and

---

6. Herbert Kaufman, *The Forest Ranger* (Baltimore: Johns Hopkins Press, 1960), pp. 207-208.

standards, the communities they work in have contrasting preferences and prejudices, and so forth. "Unchecked," Kaufman con-
cludes, "these influences could produce such diverse Ranger district programs as to dissolve the Forest Service into an aggregate
of separate entities, destroying it as an integrated, functioning
organization." [7]

How often we hear managers in business worry about the
shortcomings of the "academic," the "scientific," or the "engineering" mind in administration. Such minds are great assets,
the manager is quick to point out, but too often they show too
little interest in human relations and personnel needs. Their
training has not given them enough feel for the irrational and
emotional stresses that are continually pulling apart and wearing
down the organization and that must be ceaselessly combatted
if the organization is to survive. Of all professionals, only the
physician, perhaps, has learned at first hand how shockingly fast
an organism can deteriorate.

In his commitment to the organization, the manager regards
its welfare and survival as valuable for its *own* sake. The organization is not necessarily more important or less important than
questions of right or wrong, in his view, but it is on the scale with
other positive elements. The manager does not regard growth as
a moral process, as a series of victories of right over wrong, but as
a continuing series of accommodations, adjustments, compromises, and relationships that keep the whole agency or division
alive and operating. It is this motion, this life, to which the
managerial mind is dedicated almost above all else.

Of course, the dedicated manager never ceases to criticize the
organization and its policies when he considers it necessary. He
never ceases to hold up the ideal of what ought to be. Late in
1959, the *Harvard Business Review* ran a survey of subscribers'
feelings about "planned obsolescence." There had been a lot of
talk about the social waste and immorality of superficial model
changes, gadgets, and the like designed to make prospective

---

7. *Ibid.,* p. 87.

customers dissatisfied with their old models. HBR wanted to find out whether or not businessmen felt uneasy about it, too. A surprisingly high number of them did, often writing in blunt criticisms of the "planned obsolescence" philosophy. Yet many of these writers were men employed in firms doing the very things they criticized, and I have no doubt that most of them were working as wholeheartedly for their companies as anyone possibly could. (Their salaries and positions indicate that.)

They were putting the organization first, in other words. If in any way they were critics, theirs was a "loyal opposition." The fact that they took exception to certain policies or perhaps certain individuals in the organization in no way meant that they were any less willing to work for its survival. The masthead of *The Chicago Tribune* used to carry the slogan: "My country right or wrong, but my country" (originated by Stephen Decatur). The manager paraphrases: "My organization right or wrong, but my organization." Or, in the words of a slogan that used to be posted in Dan River Mills, "The Corporation above Self." [8]

This attitude reflects more than a practical interest in keeping a job. After all, managers are on the whole a mobile group, and a good executive can usually find other companies or agencies with different goals toward which he can work. The manager seems to obtain a kind of psychic income from serving an organization; the very fact that it exists and works is a strong point in its favor, regardless of questions about the policies it pursues. It is true that, being a manager, he is in a position to change some of the things he doesn't like, but I doubt that this hope is more than a partial explanation for his commitment. In the pattern of managers' words and actions, I sense a conviction that the organization is important *because it is*.

In such respects, the manager's way of thinking is not unlike that of the doctor's. The physician's professional interest is in making his patient healthy. Diagnosing a case in his office or at

---

8. Robert Sidney Smith, *Mill on the Dan* (Durham: Duke University Press, 1960), p. 542.

work in the operating room, he is not concerned about the virtue or social importance of his patient (although he may be at other times). It does not matter to him whether the man under the stethoscope is rich or poor, able or not able, law-abiding or criminal. It is the life, the organism that counts.

KEY DISTINCTIONS

With the foregoing points in mind we can now reflect in a more general way on the nature of this person called a manager or administrator.

First, not every person in an executive position looks at the organization in the way the manager does. There are military officers who have little or no interest in group operations; there are school superintendents who would rather be teaching in the classroom; there are business vice presidents who only get irritated at having to spend a great deal of time working through people or bringing them together. On the other hand, it should also be obvious that some people whom we think of as lawyers, doctors, or engineers are in fact administrators. The manager is commonly defined as one who gets results primarily through people, and it does not much matter whether the people wear gray flannels, interne jackets, or shop coats. In the words of one executive, who happens to be general manager of a supermarket chain:

Managers have a deep urge to mold and control the internal environment created by their industrial activity. They are passionately involved in this environment *for its own sake*—and not simply because it is also a means to a commercial end.

These facts make the manager different from the professional or technical man. The professional deals mainly with nonrecurring or unconnected individual cases—clients, patients, students, and so forth; the technician deals mainly with the application of a specific body of theoretical knowledge. When the firm of the professional or technician grows large and he spends most of his time adjusting personalities and work situations, he becomes in fact a manager.

This happens to a physician when he passes from medical practice to hospital administration, or to a teacher when he becomes a dean, or to a scientist when he goes from the laboratory to research management.[9]

In short, we are saying that the function of administration, wherever it is found and regardless of official title, can be associated with a particular point of view. How much the function creates the point of view and how much the point of view creates the function is another question that need not concern us here. It is enough to know that a significant, albeit subtle, change in outlook appears when we turn from men who are preoccupied with a skill or personal specialty to men who are concerned primarily with administering the activities of others (even though the latter may, like our research manager in the introduction, look wistfully back at their original professions). This change is clear both in what these men and women want to do and in what they actually do. The *nature* of the change is, of course, the important thing for administrators trying to describe to others what they do and for would-be administrators trying to decide if they are really interested. It is therefore the nature of the change that we want to describe in this book.

Second, the managerial mind is never perfectly realized. Its ideas are not easily practiced; they are, in fact, continually suppressed and compromised. But they are real and influential, nonetheless. If anything, the fact that the managerial mind is beyond attainment makes it more significant. Like par on a golf course, it is always being sought. It may even haunt the manager as par haunts the golfer, filling him with hope in the morning before he ventures out and with despair in the evening when he straggles home.

The manager's actions, for example, are not always consistent with his commitment to the organization. Nevertheless, this commitment will produce a pattern, an emphasis in thought and

---

9. Paul Cifrino, "The Mainspring of Business Leadership," *Harvard Business Review,* September-October, 1956, pp. 56-57.

action that is unmistakable. To use an analogy, a home-run hitter in baseball will hit singles many times, and a singles hitter will sometimes hit home runs, yet over a season the two men will have clearly contrasting hitting records. The same can be said of the administrator and the nonadministrator. Sometimes the administrator will do things inconsistent with the organization's interests (from taking too much time off to getting involved with conflicting interests), and sometimes the nonadministrator will devote more effort to administrative tasks than to his specialty. Over the long run, however, two quite different patterns of action will emerge.

Earlier I referred to the need for a theme to which there are no important exceptions. The manager's commitment to the organization gives us the core of such a theme. While there are numerous deviations from it in practice, they are due more to human failures in translating thought into action than to weakness in the motif itself.

Another point to emphasize is that the man with a managerial mind is not necessarily a "good" man or a model citizen. He may be greedy for money, he may be cynical, he may be narrow, he may be as stuffy as Willis Wayde, who planned his honeymoon so that he could talk to a certain business leader. None of these things makes much difference to our definition. After all, doctors and lawyers are sometimes greedy or cynical, too, but we still call them professionals if they meet the requirements of their work. If a doctor is in medicine partly because of the money, is he any more or less a doctor? If a lawyer has become an expert in taxation partly because of a hunger for prestige, is he any more or less a lawyer? Is there even any necessary correlation between superior managerial performance and ideals that we call socially "good"? It should not be too surprising to find that a general with a lust for power or a vice president with a craving for profit can be a better administrator—and can embody more perfectly the qualities of the administrative point of view—than a general driven by patriotic zeal or a vice president impassioned by high ideals about social organization.

Finally, we can avoid a good deal of confusion by emphasizing the distinction suggested earlier between administrators and traders. In a lecture at the Harvard Business School in 1958, Abraham Zaleznik said:

> Chester Barnard makes the point that what administrators or managers do contains both executive and nonexecutive functions. The executive functions center around the processes of decision making in groups, of organization and control of cooperation and collaboration. Nonexecutive functions consist of nonprocess actions such as making a sale, buying a commodity, preparing a "make or buy" analysis or a market survey. The role of the manager is ambiguous because persons concerned with administration, both in the worlds of business and of universities, have unclear images of the administrator. For some, the image grows out of the nonexecutive functions; for others, the executive functions. For some, the administrator is still the "wheeling and dealing" trader who comes up with a very clever idea, markets it, and makes a lot of money as a consequence.

A second writer who has emphasized the difference between administrators and nonadministrators is Ordway Tead. In his book, *The Art of Administration,* he makes these observations:

> Those who approach participation in business direction from the point of view preponderantly of "banker management," or of what Veblen called "finance capitalism," are not usually those who are deeply interested in or necessarily skilled in administration in the sense here conceived. There are still those in business who are playing for high stakes and quick results, who see industrial and mercantile enterprises as pawns in a game of financial manipulation, who are not unfairly spoken of as "business buccaneers." Promoters and "entrepreneurs" of this caliber do not tend to have administrative interests. They do not usually possess the patience, the human sensitivity and the public outlook to administer well in the constructive, long-range way today required. Fortunately the demands and occasions of present-day economic adventure lie much less in the field of financial manipulation than in the field of the more sober and steady building of productive unity on foundations of cooperative effort.[10]

10. Ordway Tead, *The Art of Administration* (New York: McGraw-Hill Book Company, Inc., 1951), p. 198.

Value Added by Administration

Marketing men have a concept that they call "value added by distribution." It refers to the value to the consumer of having goods where he wants them, when he wants them, and in the quantities he wants. In other words, it is not enough from the consumer's point of view that good products are made somewhere from carefully purchased materials, that parts are engineered well and manufactured skillfully. It is also important that these products and services be in the right markets at the right times—and in sufficient quantity to meet the need. If you want a power mower in the summer and can't find one for sale, it is little solace to learn that the stores were full of them last winter.

A similar important assumption of the managerial mind seems to be that of "value added by administration." In this view a productive organization consists of more than the number of people in it, their skills, their motivations, their equipment. A productive organization is made up of the right people at the right places at the right times with the right purposes and equipment. This means goals that are understood, directions that are accepted, arguments that are settled, breakdowns that are fixed up. Value added by administration is what keeps things moving. It is the X factor that, when added to men and materials, accounts for the organization's capacity to operate and renew itself.

This factor has long fascinated students and analysts. It cannot be broken down like a machine into parts and functions. It cannot be measured like elements in a time and motion study. Viewed precisely, mechanically, analytically, the administrator's role may seem elusive and even parasitical. But to the manager, at least, the need is great and ever-present.

If critics think of the administrator's job as being superimposed—an extra layer on top of the layers of people who *do* things—the manager replies that nevertheless the job is essential. If the economist writes of organizations as if they were brought into being automatically by markets or statutes, the manager can point out that there are plenty of cases on record of organizations creating markets and rules but none of markets creating organizations. Only people can do that. If the lawyer looks at the work group in terms of rights and duties, the manager answers that rights and duties are important but that they do not by themselves live or make anything go. If the philosopher tries to hold the organization to moral precepts, the manager answers that morality does not make an operation run either. If the legislator cries for business to pay staggering taxes or for prosecution of a staggering number of antitrust suits, the manager reminds him that the organization must serve itself before it can serve others.

A good deal more than administrative dedication is needed, however, to assure productivity and growth. As a matter of fact, the manager's sense of commitment can, if he lets it carry him too far, become his own worst enemy. At this point, our story begins to grow complicated, and we turn to certain dilemmas that beset the managerial mind. First, however, let us pause to look at some general implications of this chapter.

IMPLICATIONS FOR INDIVIDUALS

Earlier in this book, we considered certain questions that practicing managers, would-be managers, and others have about the quality of the managerial mind. How does the manager's commitment to the organization bear on these questions?

1. *The man or woman going into administration from a field like engineering, law, or accountancy will recognize that, as before, personal interests must be subordinated to the interests of a larger group.* There are, to be sure, real qualitative differences between "organization-mindedness" and the kind of "cause-mindedness" characteristic of leading professions. Yet the former has the same effect as the latter in increasing the demand for standards, for knowledge, for a sense of tradition. In all of these

respects, the administrative point of view must be sharply distinguished from those of men in commerce and politics who put *private* profit first in their thinking as a matter of principle.

2. *The person going into managerial work from a student, commercial, or other nonprofessional background will probably find it necessary to "conform" more than before.* The experience should, however, be different only in detail from what he would encounter on going into a profession. (This issue will be discussed at some length in Chapter 3 and in later sections.)

3. *The commitment to the organization makes disciplined thinking necessary.* There must be consistency, method, predictability; opportunism must not be allowed to dominate. For instance, it is predictable that the administrator will concern himself with the development of successors, even though training people is not his forte, and it is predictable that the administrator will concern himself with budget matters, even though he may not personally enjoy figures and quantitative analysis. In comparison, lawyers and doctors dutifully "keep up" in areas outside their main interests too. Here again the managerial mind demonstrates both professional and philosophical qualities. An engineer, doctor, or teacher turning to administration as a career will find rigors of the same nature as those that characterized his original profession, although differing in type and degree. But an entrepreneur or "one-man-show" operator may well find the administrative approach too full of restrictions for his liking; it may make him feel "hemmed in" and unable to move as freely and unpredictably as he has grown used to. And a person preoccupied with matters of status rather than performance may find the yardsticks of his bosses an endless source of frustration.

4. *It may well be a mistake for leading managers to explain what they are trying to do in terms only of bringing home a paycheck, performing a public service, making a profit, etc.* Why not bluntly acknowledge—and proudly—that they value their organizations *per se,* as physicians are articulate about the value they attach to human life, whether a particular life is "good" or

"bad"? An appealing case for this aspect of the managerial mind could be made to the public because the public, as we shall note in the last chapter, has more and more reason to revere organizational life.

5. *A young person considering management as a career (in contrast to selling, accounting, or a staff specialty, for example) would do well to ask himself if he is the kind of person who can develop enthusiasm for an organization.* Is he the kind who can find fulfillment in serving a department, bureau, or division as some people find satisfaction in making a big sale, solving a financial problem, or working for a public cause? If he is not, he may still be successful in a material way as an executive. He may be so capable that he will succeed at almost anything at which he tries his hand. But he will probably be troubled by feelings of ambivalence, because he will see the importance of organizational interests but not be able to *feel* their importance. Unable to identify himself with the organization, yet sensing the need for such identification, he may then become one of those unhappy individuals who wake up one day to discover, too late, that they have traveled the wrong road to work satisfaction.

6. *In business, corporate managers are sometimes led to act in ways contrary to the long-run interests of stockholders.* For instance, they may spend much time and money on diversifying the products and services offered, so that the long-term survival of the firm is better assured; whereas investors would be better served if the company "put all its eggs in one basket," made the most of the market while it lasted, and liquidated when profits began to run out. Again, the managerial mind tends to favor retained earnings over long-term debt as a source of funds, whereas the opposite order of preference would be in the investors' interest. (For a full analysis of such conflicts, see Gordon Donaldson's article, "Financial Goals: Management vs. Stockholders." [11])

---

11. *Harvard Business Review*, May-June 1963, p. 116.

2

DILEMMAS

OF

THE

MANAGERIAL

MIND

THERE ARE PROBLEMS on the managerial mind, as a result of its commitment to the organization. They shape it and color it, and give it added dimension as surely as, down through the ages, certain problems of law and justice have shaped the legal mind and certain problems concerning the aims of science have affected the scientific mind. I refer, of course, not to everyday operating problems or the endless frictions and difficulties of "keeping the shop going," important as they may be, but to basic and chronic problems, those that arise from the very nature of the attitudes and aspirations of the manager.

Too Little Influence or Too Much?

First, there is the problem of influence. The administrator must achieve influence over people if he is to satisfy his aspirations for the organization.

From time to time in the past, this problem has been formulated in negative terms by writers and observers; that is, they have emphasized the manager's inadequacy in directing human affairs. Managers and their biographers only delude themselves, we have been told, in thinking that managerial leadership can have a profound impact on a complex organization. Leo Tolstoy played on this theme through much of *War and Peace*. Here, for example, is a telling commentary on the Russian General Kutuzov's preparations for the battle of Borodino, a decisive event in the defeat of Napoleon's invasion of 1812:

> Learned military authorities quite seriously tell us that Kutuzov should have moved his army to the Kaluga road long before reaching Fili, and that somebody actually submitted such a proposal to him. But a commander in chief, especially at a difficult moment, has always before him not one proposal but dozens simultaneously. And all these proposals, based on strategies and tactics, contradict each other.
>
> A commander in chief's business, it would seem, is simply to choose one of these projects. But even that he cannot do. Events and time do not wait. For instance, on the twenty-eighth it is suggested to him to cross to the Kaluga road, but just then an adjutant gallops up from Miloradovich asking whether he is to engage the French or retire. An order must be given him at once, that instant. And the order to retreat carries us past the turn to the Kaluga road. And after the adjutant comes the commissary general asking where the stores are to be taken, and the chief of the hospitals asks where the wounded are to go, and a courier from Petersburg brings a letter from the sovereign which does not admit of the possibility of abandoning Moscow, and the commander in chief's rival, the man who is undermining him (and there are always not merely one but several such), presents a new project diametrically opposed to that of turning to the Kaluga road, and the commander in chief himself needs sleep and refreshment to maintain his energy, and a respectable general who has been overlooked in the distribution of

rewards comes to complain, and the inhabitants of the district have to be defended, and an officer sent to inspect the locality comes in and gives a report quite contrary to what was said by the officer previously sent; and a spy, a prisoner, and a general who has been on reconnaisance, all describe the position of the enemy's army differently.

People accustomed to misunderstand or to forget these inevitable conditions of a commander in chief's actions describe to us, for instance, the position of the army at Fili and assume that the commander in chief could, on the first of September, quite freely decide whether to abandon Moscow or defend it; whereas, with the Russian army less than four miles from Moscow, no such question existed.[1]

This problem is real; certainly the administrator is often frustrated in his aims. Yet it seems to me that today he is more concerned, at least in his thoughtful moments, with precisely the opposite problem. He *does* direct, control, and influence people in his organization. Indeed, consciously or subconsciously, he worries about the possibility of his power being exercised *too* successfully.

Why does this danger exist? There are several reasons. There is the growing need for more smoothly functioning and better co-ordinated organizations in the modern world. Managers have sought, with increasing success, to extend their influence over other people, both in scope and in intensity. In recent generations, they have expanded and refined management's traditional power over jobs, promotions, and salaries. Jobs have been more precisely defined, promotions have been more clearly graded, salaries have been tied with greater accuracy to performance. Furthermore, while leaders have always been skilled in shaping the images and aspirations that guide men in groups, these skills have grown enormously in the twentieth century: The executive has not only become a better communicator thanks to new techniques, but he has had better "feedback" from his audiences to guide him in tactics and strategy. Management has also developed

---

1. Leo Tolstoy, *War and Peace* (New York: Oxford University Press, 1933), translated by Louise and Aylmer Maude.

numerous analytical techniques for diagnosing the strengths and weaknesses of an organization. These techniques, ranging from psychological tests to data processing, have contributed more than tremendous adjutant staffs to making command more sensitive, perceptive, and efficient. At the same time, people have grown more dependent on organizations and more used to them, so that the mood of the times also favors greater management influence.

But here is the difficulty. The very attempt of the manager to keep his organization growing by directing it effectively is partly self-defeating, for he must impose restrictions on other people, and restrictions on them sooner or later become restrictions on himself.

THE INEFFICIENCY OF EFFICIENCY

This dilemma is built into the very basis of managerial authority. Its consequences are to be seen daily in the operation of almost every agency or enterprise, and managers stumble over them—not out of stupidity or forgetfulness but because they can't avoid them. Let us review some typical problems.

Subjugation of personality. For one thing, management has a "depersonalizing" influence. When the manager asks employees to perform a task and expects them to do it satisfactorily, he is using them as means to an end. It does not matter that they are working for him by choice or that the task is necessary. The fact is that they are doing particular jobs at particular times because, in one way or another, *he* told them to. And so, clearly, there is a certain restriction of free will, of personality (even though great administrative gains are made). This restriction tends to create—unless countermeasures are taken—a vicious cycle in which the subjugation of personality increases, and the more it increases the more vulnerable management and the organization become.

Consultants, among others, are all too familiar with this phenomenon—and it does not matter how well managed their client firms are. A machine operator is asked, "Why are you doing the job in that way?" He answers, "Because the foreman wants me to." A research supervisor is asked, "How many of your people are doing basic research?" He answers, "The boss thinks we should have everybody working on product improvement." It is not his policy but somebody else's. An organization may expect satisfactory work from men with such attitudes, but it will not arouse the high degree of personal involvement and resourcefulness that it needs for maximum growth. When trouble comes, as sooner or later it must, management is tempted to "bear down," which means to use employees as means to ends more than before. The drain on personnel resources thus increases. The end result is the familiar spectacle of the firm or agency that is full of "dead wood."

Propagation of errors. Administrators know that their own errors tend to go uncorrected. To illustrate, a supervisor who has spent ten years in one plant changes to a job in another plant and brings with him certain attitudes learned on the old job that are inappropriate to the new one. He can inject these attitudes into the new operation because he has power to direct and control. Through management, errors can thus be spread and nurtured. A similar case is that of the law-school dean who does his job so well that what was once a small enrollment becomes a large one. The new situation calls for changed leadership, and the dean knows he should change his "one-man-show" ways, but he can't adjust completely. His ways become increasingly unrealistic, but he can enforce them through management. The same problem often arises in government when a new set of conditions arises. The managers of the affected bureau continue to apply the old standards, with the result that the more effective their control, the more inviting the bureau becomes for the legislative axe. One could go on at length with such illustrations.

Underutilization of human resources. Another kind of difficulty arises when subordinates must use "second-hand" thinking. By definition, the manager gets results through other people, yet he must instruct them on the basis of his own experience. His judgment or his way of doing the job may be excellent, but a subordinate may have trouble using it. An employee may claim that when he has an administrative problem he always follows a certain rule: "I ask myself first if there isn't a policy for cases like this, and ten to one there is." But of course the authors of the policy couldn't possibly have anticipated each exact situation, and even if they had they might be horrified at his interpretation. All they could hope to do would be to develop uniform standards and some consistency in the way ideas are carried out.

Thus, in the interests of good administration, the policymakers have sacrificed some of the organization's potential. For when employees rely on policy—on someone else's experience—for problem solving, they may necessarily have to ignore their own experience. It is not surprising that some notable cases of "hardening of the policies" in government and industry have occurred even in organizations staffed with bright men: If men must sacrifice too much of their own initiative for the sake of policy, then the organization will be deprived of the fresh ideas and flexible thinking it needs to remain dynamic.

All the difficulties just described combine to affect the manager as well as the managed. Consciously or unconsciously, he knows that he is restricting others, that errors in his thinking go uncorrected, and that he is wasting abilities by trying to harness them. Even though his organization may be doing satisfactorily compared to other organizations, he may well be concerned. He has reason to fear that no matter how smooth the surface seems, it can begin crumbling at any time. He is often nagged by anxiety, wondering when the breakdown will happen. Such anxiety has a way of communicating itself surreptitiously to others—to say nothing of the wearing effect on himself.

Perhaps he tries to solve the problem by being more efficient, by exerting greater control. Paradoxically, however, the more he succeeds, the further he falls short of his goal, for, openly or secretively, his employees feel more strongly that they are being "used" and resist him more firmly. Their defenses range from little lapses and silly mistakes to the "slowdown" and, in extreme cases (a conquered country, for example), assassination and revolt. Of course, not all his people will resist him, but the ones who don't are the faithful automatons who, while capable of carrying out routines, contribute little of the vitality and resourcefulness the organization needs to survive.

What about the organization? The drains on its effectiveness are most pronounced of all. Recently I heard the chief executive of a famous American company rate the effectiveness of his organization at a little over 10 per cent (obtained by multiplying his ratings of three main corporate functions). The rating was only an informed guess, he said, but it was as likely to be too high as too low. While he aimed to improve that figure, it is significant that his corporation is considered by other businessmen, business educators, and investors to be well managed. Whatever its effectiveness, I doubt that many other companies and agencies are doing much better.

The fact that over-all organizational effectiveness is so low surely reflects the chronic problems previously described.

CONFLICTS OF INTEREST

The inefficiency of efficiency is not the only dilemma in the administrative point of view. Some problems take the form of conflicts *with* the feeling of commitment to the organization.

Confused loyalties. Take, for example, the problem of personal loyalty. Once upon a time it may not have been perplexing. Life at work, as well as at home, was usually far simpler. The administrator in the medieval church could be fairly sure that he would serve one church—and probably in one place—all his life. The head of a nineteenth-century forge, although he may have had to struggle to survive, was likely to be working where his father had worked before him and where his sons would work after him. The manager of a mine could easily spend so much of the day in the operations area and be so absorbed in it that little else of a business nature crossed his mind.

Today, by contrast, the manager's life typically spreads over a far wider area. There are many possibilities for changing jobs, as well as for changing areas and assignments. As his life has become more complicated and the possibilities more various, the manager has become less sure how to allocate his loyalties and how to resolve the conflicts among them. His *general* feeling of commitment to organizational interests may be deep and strong, but he does not feel exclusively and permanently committed to any one unit. Learned, Ulrich, and Booz have described the conflict that may result:

Whatever a man's personal feelings were in the Farwell Company, membership in the top management group also implied an intense loyalty to the company. A man's behavior might be judged more than anything else by whether, in countless large or small ways, he reflected this loyalty in his actions. Clashes between personalities and personal ambitions were expected to remain subordinate to the interests of the concern itself. The more a man observed the outward codes and practices of loyal behavior, the more deeply he might come to believe in them. Thus the code of loyalty tended to be self-reinforcing. Yet many executives in the company had strong personal ambitions, and it was not considered improper that they should. Hence many individuals faced a dilemma. Men who perceived that their personal objectives ran counter to the interests of the men around them were likely to feel a deep sense of guilt and conflict, no matter what course their actions took. In one case, for example, an executive who decided to leave his company for a higher position elsewhere felt deep pangs of conscience for "letting down" his colleagues.[2]

Such feelings of guilt would not arise, of course, if the administrator did not feel strong commitment to the organization in the

---

2.   Edmund P. Learned, David N. Ulrich, and Donald R. Booz, *Executive Action* (Boston: Division of Research, Harvard Business School, 1951), pp. 48-49.

first place. In a real sense, therefore, the managerial mind has "brought this problem on itself."

The countervailing spirit. Then, too, there is the problem of personal values, which can create as great a tension as the conflict of loyalties, if not greater. The manager finds himself spending much of his time fighting for success, and success demands meeting schedules and being punctual and "getting along." As he finds himself pacing others, so he too is paced. The clock determines when an appointment ends. The calendar determines his freedom to explore a new idea or to visit with an unexpected caller. The never-ending need for efficiency determines much of what he thinks about. Often there is no escape from it even at the country club or at home.

Yet, no matter how well the administrator follows the dictates of efficiency, there is a part of him that yearns to be careless and to daydream, to visit without watching the clock and to follow a fancy now and then. This instinct has been nourished in his childhood and reinforced by the liberal arts tradition, and his memories keep reminding him that there is more —or should be more—to life than meeting schedules and "getting along." And so there is an inner conflict between yearner and earner, between dreamer and scheduler, and it is not always resolved in favor of the organization.

In short, the manager does not always act "like a manager should," and my point is that his behavior may not result from a failure in his emotional control or from simple human error but from inconsistent values within the managerial mind itself. The stronger one value (the organization, efficiency), the stronger another may have to be (revolt against efficiency) in order to be preserved.

It is for this reason perhaps that isolated acts offer little help in appraising the extent of a man's commitment to the organization. The fact that on this occasion or that he "told the whole place to go to hell," indulged in an orgy of wasteful spending, or picked a fight with someone merely for the sake of fighting means little if examined out of context. The test is in the pattern —whether or not the *prevailing* motive appears to be to further the interests of the work group or enterprise.

Other-directedness. Another dilemma involves personal reward. Working hard and intelligently for the success of an organization does not guarantee a manager promotion or acclaim, and of course it does not guarantee power or profits to the organization either. His administrative decisions are only part of his decision-making responsibility, and, in addition, there are unpredictables—bosses who are themselves not good enough managers to appreciate the virtues of other managers, political reverses, economic changes, and many more. There is an almost irresistible tendency therefore for a manager to "hedge his bets" by meeting other standards of success, whether or not they are consistent with the organization's needs.

The more he values the success standards of other people, however, the less satisfying he is likely to find commitment to the organization, for most people do not put organizational needs on a par with personal wealth, prestige, comfort, or popularity. Ideally, the managerial mind views service to the organization as its own reward; such service does not save a person from pain, suffering, and defeat in the world, but it is satisfying *per se*. Such martyrdom, however, is likely to make more sense in theory than in practice.

The conflict takes on added significance because the administrative view is not always the best view, and commitment to an agency or enterprise is not the only commitment worth making. If, for example, a government administrator is faced with a choice between sacrificing a political goal for the sake of the welfare of his bureau or sacrificing the organization for the goal, the decision may be difficult, no matter how dedicated he is. The fact that winning votes for the party, advancement to higher office, public power, and similar aims appeal to his "other-directed" self does not make them bad. Similarly, a research director may consider departing from his established policy of seeking balanced, long-term growth for his organization in order to concentrate on perfecting a certain product or process that no one else has been able to develop. The fact that success will put him in an engineering "hall of fame" does not make his decision reprehensible. There is sometimes wisdom in progress for progress's sake, even when it jeopardizes a department's security and well being.

Doing vs. supervising. Finally, and in some ways most frustrating of all, there is the problem of the manager who overshadows his assistants. Many an agency administrator can write a better brief than the assistant to whom the job is entrusted; many a senior bank officer can size up a credit risk better than the person whose full-time responsibility it is. What is more, in almost every organization, there are likely to be older managers who are wiser and tougher than the young men they hire and who see, almost every day, instances of weakness or temerity that seem to them exasperating. This attitude will develop no matter how carefully the new men are selected or how nearly they represent the "cream of the crop." Dean Stanley F. Teele has remarked:

As I observe managers at work, I am struck by the fact that there are large numbers who have all the intellectual capacity to analyze and to reach conclusions. What they lack is the courage, the fortitude, to turn these intellectual conclusions into wise decisions. If I had to pick a single reason for men failing to make the most of themselves, it would be this lack of courage and ability to make wise decisions.[3]

Seeing a man falter for such a reason, the senior naturally finds it hard not to step in and take over personally, especially since he is interested in the results of the day's work. Once he does, however, he reduces his scope as a manager. The very fact that he must administer means that he must curtail some of the contributions he might make to the enterprise.

---

3. Stanley F. Teele, "H.B.S. and the Future," October 4, 1960 (privately distributed).

UNDERSTANDING THE PROBLEM

Where does this brief run-down of dilemmas and problems leave us? We have seen that the administrator's commitments to the organization are not easy to fulfill because direction and control tend in part to defeat the very purposes they are intended to serve—the security, growth, and vitality of the organization. Furthermore, an administrator's dedication to his department or enterprise may stir up in him competing values that also need to be served if he is to maintain a balanced outlook—such values as personal advancement, the need to rebel sometimes against deadening efficiency, and the satisfaction of working for "causes" instead of organizations.

There are, it seems to me, at least two morals that can be drawn from examination of these conflicts. First, administration is a subject that cannot be broken down into neat formulas. This point seems obvious enough, yet it bears repeating because of the continuing flood of easy-to-follow prescriptions for success.

Second, while the administrative point of view is not a model of logic and consistency, it may strike some observers as being fuller of inconsistencies than it really is. This is because administrators are always balancing conflicting needs and pressures in many different ways. If the observer does not look beyond the vagaries of knowledge and experience possessed by a manager, he is not likely to see the pattern I am trying to describe in this book. To illustrate from personal experience:

In the Navy during World War II, I worked with two officers who were as different in temperament as could be. Both were good managers. They both got work done through other people, yet one delegated freely, the other very little. On the surface at least, the example demonstrates a lack of pattern in management thinking. Yet in each officer's mind, I know, were the same dedication to the divisional organization and many of the other values and attitudes to be described in later chapters.

Two teachers of business administration whom I know have quite different kinds of knowledge and experience, and they are wont to interpret knowledge differently. One believes that a man-

ager should stay strictly at the policy-making level in his conferences with juniors; the other departs from "the book" frequently
and even sees wisdom in the manager's getting down to the smallest
operating details from time to time. Again, on the surface, the
example seems to prove lack of consistency in the managerial mind.
Yet, in my observation, both teachers value the basic pattern of attitudes outlined in this book. It is at the level of knowledge and
day-to-day judgment that they differ.

Managers have long sought to understand their dilemmas
and to cope with them. Their efforts deserve careful examination,
for they have many implications for management and society
alike. Beginning with the next chapter, therefore, we shall consider a series of attitudes and approaches that represent the manager's attempt to meet the problems of organization as effectively
as possible. His success has, it seems to me, been extraordinary.
If we have failed to appreciate it, our failure may have been due
in part to our lack of a valid rationale for explaining his accomplishment (writers have found it easier to explain his failures)
and in part to our forgetfulness of the enormous problems with
which he contends.

IMPLICATIONS FOR INDIVIDUALS

How do the dilemmas and problems of administration bear
on attempts to rank the managerial mind with other "minds"?

1. *It should be recognized that such personal qualities as
courage, integrity, good will, and capacity for hard work—while
important—are no more the whole story of effectiveness in management than in science, politics, journalism, or any other major
field.* What is necessary is a unique way of *thinking* about administration—a general intellectual approach. Books and lectures
that try to distill the secrets of management success in ten words,
three qualities, or one rule give a badly distorted picture.

2. *The would-be administrator should be prepared to find
managerial life a crucible of conflicting social values in our demo-*

cratic culture. He will not find administrative thinking dominated by such neat, orderly, parochial sets of assumptions about management behavior as the statement that "the business manager manipulates men and materials to maximize profits"—as if he thought of nothing else. Rather, he will find managers bringing to decision-making—sometimes directly, sometimes indirectly— almost all their social, cultural, and religious values. While these values do not always fare well when pitted against the manager's commitment to the organization, some of the most tenacious fighting on their behalf goes on in administrative councils—because such conflicts are built into administrative situations and because our manager is by definition one who works through people.

3. *The administrator needs a way of looking at life, as well as at organizational problems.* The man who considers moving into administration as a career would do well to ask himself some hard questions. "Am I the kind of person who can live in a world of tangled interests, or would I do better in areas where there is a relatively high degree of order and consistency?" "Do I have the physical and emotional capacity to survive conflicts concerning social, cultural, and moral values?" "Have I the willingness and capacity to be tough with people when I have to be?" (As we have seen, management means a certain loss of initiative and self-fulfillment for subordinates. The executive who is too sensitive to these drains could become too "nice" to achieve organizational goals.)

3

THE

IMPORTANCE

OF

NONCONFORMITY

IN CONTEMPORARY SOCIETY, the individual is under strong pressures to conform to the behavior and belief patterns set by groups. Organizational life is no exception. Things run more smoothly if quarrels can be kept to a minimum. Time lost in arguments can be reduced if points of difference can be glossed over. Particularly if the manager puts the organization first in his thinking, the temptation to develop unity of opinion on various problems is strong. All these pressures have been described many times by writers, some of whom have even advocated yielding to them.

But the managerial mind stops working when it gives in to pressures to conform. Once the administrator's thinking merges with the thinking of others in the organization, once his own thoughts and values lose their importance, he can no longer manage effectively. What can he contribute—beside another indistinguishable voice—if he brings no individual point of view to the firm? How can he provide direction for others if he sees an issue only as the group sees it? How can he expect his employees to work creatively as a group unless they think and act differently from one another?

The high value placed on differences—differences among individuals as well as among groups—is one of the most important characteristics of the managerial mind. It is not the friend but the enemy of the so-called organization man, at least in so far as that term implies molded opinion. The fact of the matter is that the "organization man" could not begin to cope effectively with the dilemmas outlined in the previous chapter.

One reason why observers have exaggerated the prevalence of the so-called "organization man" is their failure to distinguish between the internal and external aspects of organization. Externally there is no doubt that conformity is commonly encouraged for purposes of expediency. It is said, for example, that Ford Motor Company would like to have all its dealers in cities and towns look and act about the same, so that "Ford" will mean the same thing to everyone; again, the military establishment is famed for its efforts to standardize the public relations activities of its officers. But this sort of thing should not be confused with the internal side of administration, which is what we are concerned about in this chapter since that is where the more universal qualities of the managerial mind function. Here we have quite a different story. For instance, two automobile dealers who advertise their showrooms in the same way, emphasize neatness, and maintain that "the customer is always right" may have radically different ways of developing salesmen, employ assistants with widely varying temperaments, ideals, and notions about business, and follow other contrasting patterns of administration.

A number of valid reasons for encouraging differences can be distinguished.

People and ideas at first distrusted or even hated are often found later to be essential. Such discoveries will never be made, of course, if the object of suspicion is eliminated at the start.

This insight is an old one and as difficult as ever to apply. Time after time an administrator has found that a suggestion he had rejected—or wanted to reject—was precisely what was needed. A government bureau with traditionally conservative policies bitterly resists adopting more liberal goals, yet, as the public becomes restless, the latter turn out to be necessary to survival. Officials in a company dominated by scientists and engineers despise the marketing research man, until they discover that he has the additional ingredient most needed for long-term growth. The college administration steeped in traditional teaching methods looks down its nose at audio-visual aids and other new devices, which later prove to be of great worth and significance. In such cases, differences have an intellectual value even though they cause personal discomfort.

Dealing with contrasting views adds to the interest of the manager's job. If his own thinking is different from that of others in his department or division and if they also differ among themselves, the whole work atmosphere is more challenging and stimulating. Such an atmosphere can mean a great deal to an intelligent, restless, ambitious man. Indeed, it is revealing to note to what lengths of self-denial and restraint some executives will go in order to force subordinates to be individualistic. Here are some observations on "Mr. Wood," a vice president of the "Trygil Company":

Wood had long since learned not to throw off any chance remarks which could take on the color of subtle directives. He could be spontaneous about a matter once he had tested the ground he was walking on, but a sixth sense told him when he was reaching the limits. For example, in discussing a problem a junior had brought to him which suggested several possible courses of action, Wood took care not to indicate his own preference and thereby limit the junior's thinking. He could show an interest and throw off ideas of his own without attaching special importance to them. Usually, he reserved his spontaneity for matters not immediately connected with business, except when he was talking to a few of his closest associates who were in no danger of misunderstanding him. Some of his subordinates thought he was rather cool, but he paid this price willingly to avoid causing them confusion. . . .

In spite of his surface detachment, the temptation to tell other people how to do things was one that Wood felt almost all the time. He usually had a good sense of what should be done, but even more important, he had a deep and lively sense of "style," which had developed out of his own working habits, and of course he liked seeing things done in his own style better than any other. Much of his effectiveness came from his capacity to resist this temptation. He had realized, between his 45th and 50th years, that the satisfaction of letting other men learn often outweighed, in the long run, the satisfaction of doing things himself.[1]

The organization as a whole is more likely to come alive with new insights and ideas. More centers of initiative are likely to develop. In the case study just mentioned, the authors drop some telling hints from time to time of what an aggressive, live-wire organization "Mr. Wood" headed. This is a typical result where management welcomes differences.

Our managerial society is full of executives and supervisors taking such an attitude. In case after case, the high quality of their work is dependent on their close association with men of sharply contrasting dispositions. Take the case of John Ernst-hausen, President of the Norwalk Truck Line Company, and his sales manager, Charles Hoke:

Each of these two men are strong personalities. Each tends to complement the other, and each counterbalances the other's weaknesses. John will be brusque with a terminal manager; Charlie will go out and smooth the ruffled feelings. Charlie will jump on a dispatcher for failure to deliver promptly—John will salve the wounded pride. Each is, in turn, the greatest booster in the industry for the other. Both are brutally frank with each other, and often the "fur flies" when they discuss a thorny point. But each, in turn, is a safety valve for the other; instead of holding feelings, they fly with

---

1.   Edmund P. Learned, David N. Ulrich, and Donald R. Booz, *Executive Action* (Boston: Division of Research, Harvard Business School, 1951), p. 96.

full force, and any ill feelings potentially building up are automatically dissipated in the process. John is essentially conservative; the lessons of childhood and the early jobs were well learned. Charlie is optimistic and bombastic in his plans; in John's words, "Charlie would build a truck line around the world if he got half a chance." John's conservatism is particularly evidenced when a new or changed method is proposed. John almost uniformly desires the "tried" method, and is a difficult man to convince on any innovation. Charlie is ever the innovator. New techniques, new ideas, new facilities are promoted by Charlie with great zeal. When an equal portion of these two men's views is drafted, the end product tends to be a stable, middle-of-the-road approach that has given the Company its steady, balanced growth over the years.[2]

Individuals gain perspective. Neither the manager nor anyone else can compare what he thinks and why he thinks it with other people's thinking until he can find out what that thinking is. Obviously he will come by this knowledge more easily in an atmosphere where differences are respected. The more freely he can test, match, and compare his views with those of others, the more opportunities he has for evaluating his own strengths and weaknesses (with all that means for developing self-confidence), as well as for sizing up the capacities of the organization. Not surprisingly, some executives who despise committees as decision-making groups nevertheless make use of them for their value in self-education.

Indeed, the higher the level of judgment required, the more difficult it becomes to check out an idea *except* by resort to a different way of thinking. Good executives seem to act instinctively on this proposition in policy-making. The procedure is both a help in making good decisions and a source of personal reassurance. It is not so important in technical projects and routine operations because there the validity of a decision can generally be appraised quickly and objectively by the manager himself. But the higher or more general the level of judgment required,

---

2. Wayne G. Broehl, Jr., *Trucks . . . Trouble . . . and Triumph: The Norwalk Truck Line Company* (New York: Prentice-Hall, Inc., 1954), pp. 196-197.

and especially the more it involves subjective appraisals—of desirable organizational goals, progress toward goals, the threat of critics or competitors, the state of public opinion, economic conditions, and similar questions—the more impossible it becomes for an executive to test an opinion by objective criteria. The eminent British manager and lawyer, Sir Geoffrey Vickers, has made this point well, distinguishing carefully between three levels of judgment, which he has termed "action," "reality," and "value judgments." [3]

The manager often finds it valuable—perhaps indispensable—to turn to other persons in order to decide on the validity of a judgment he is entertaining. Ideally, he turns to the man who is as intelligent as he is but who usually reaches conclusions by entirely different mental processes. If the manager tends, for example, to be logical and orderly in his thinking, he may discuss an opinion with an associate or acquaintance who tends to be impressionistic and intuitive. While the latter may have a quite different notion of the problem, in discussion he can still provide the special reactions or arguments necessary to confirm or reject the idea in question. More interesting still, if the manager is a man who relies on the faculty of visual imagination in decision-making, he may look for a respected man who makes practically no use whatever of that gift, and vice versa. At least one expert has suggested that equally intelligent people often make equally intelligent decisions with exactly opposite uses of the faculty of visual imagination.[4]

Lonely Thinker

It is true that some important requirements of organizational life call for managers to conform in certain respects. Profits must

---

3. Sir Geoffrey Vickers, "Judgment," *The Manager*, January, 1961, p. 30.

4. D. W. Grey Walter, *The Living Brain* (London: Duckworth, 1953), p. 152. Cited by Vickers, *loc. cit.*

be stressed in business, good relations with taxpayers in school administration, conformity of dress in the military. In any organization, there must be agreement that policies and decisions, once made, will be respected in action. We must not forget, however, that there are also strong natural influences toward individuality of thought.

For one thing, a certain amount of loneliness accompanies the position of manager. A field examiner for a government agency is made head of the St. Louis office and can no longer share in much of the easy camaraderie he once had with clerks and other examiners. The head of a local union is promoted to the national executive offices, where he must now deal at arm's length with his old friends in the local. An operator is promoted to foreman and can no longer gripe freely about "management" or sympathize readily with a worker who has been lazy and needs discipline. A corporate vice president is elected president by the board of directors and finds he no longer has anyone in whom to confide. In the words of one close observer:

> The president has to live alone and like it. If he indulges in the luxury of thinking out loud, he sets off a chain reaction of rumors throughout the organization. He is the final, focal point of all the competitive pressures of men in the organization who are ambitious. If he confides in one and not in the others, he immediately lowers the morale of his executive staff. . . .
>
> Most company presidents show an immediate understanding of what President William Howard Taft had in mind when he said after he had been in the White House several months, "Nobody ever drops in for the evening." [5]

Furthermore, whether the special attributes that make a good executive are possessed by one man in ten, one man in a hundred, or one man in ten thousand, the fact remains that he is likely to be "different" to begin with, or he never would have striven to become a manager. He certainly will be different after he has been in supervision for a while. After all, the angle of view varies

---

5. J. Elliott Janney, "Company Presidents Look at Themselves," *Harvard Business Review*, May-June, 1952, pp. 61, 62.

greatly from job to job and level to level, highlighting different facts, ranges of facts, and goals. Managers look at situations from different points in the organization from those of their subordinates. In addition, they are likely to emphasize different results. A magazine publisher, for instance, may worry about an issue's effect on the renewal rate, while the art editor focuses simply on attracting attention and readership. Managers may also perceive different information about a specific problem. A bureau head, for instance, receives first-hand reports from Washington, but one of his assistants may hear only from subordinates in a certain division. Finally, managers have different people to please. A factory manager, for instance, may lie awake nights worrying about the owner's ideas, while the head accountant in the plant need only please the treasurer.

To widen the gulf still further between men in different jobs at different levels, the more power and authority a manager has over people, the more frequently he must make arguable choices. An intelligence analyst in Washington is concerned with methods of getting accurate data, and these methods can be objectively checked in a number of ways. In contrast, the director of a branch office is also concerned with achieving correct information, but he has only judgment and intuition to guide him. Similarly, a time-study supervisor in a textile plant can test the figures his staff comes up with and prove them "right." But once he becomes head of the plant, he may have to decide whether to move it from the Ohio town where it has always been to a low-cost area in the South, and there are a multitude of pros and cons. If he decides in favor of the move, the stockholders (and probably the financial executives) will be happy because profits will probably increase, but the Ohio community (and probably the public relations director) will never forgive him because of resulting unemployment.

The controversies created by such choices have a profound impact on the psychology of the administrator. At the minimum, he must articulate his reasons for adopting one course of action rather than another; at the maximum, he must become reflective and self-analytical. In either case, he must extend the range of his own abilities and increase his knowledge—with the inevitable result that today he is not only likely to be different in outlook from his associates but from what he himself was only yesterday.

Values, standards, goals, and assumptions—these factors deepen differences of opinion as one thinks about them. And as differences grow, the manager finds himself less capable of seeing problems as his associates do. Increasingly, his primary identification tends to be with the organization—which acts as a kind of third force. The managerial mind thus brings executives closer to the organization than to each other, and, since the organization's only meaning lies in the mind of the man who serves it, the result is to increase individuality still further.

I remember the way a young corporation executive once described his boss to me: "Lots of times he's out of phase with us. When we're down, he'll be up. When we're up, he'll be worrying about things that might happen. He's never satisfied. When we're discouraged, he'll be a beacon of hope. But when we're proud of ourselves for something we've done, that's when he'll go around needling people. . . . " Such an executive often conveys the impression of having unusual capacity to see beyond the problems of the moment. Some observers may even attribute spiritual qualities to him. They may see him as profoundly influencing others while he himself remains comparatively unaffected by them, as if his own attitudes and aspirations spring from a fresh and different source.

It is no wonder that, at his best, he frequently inspires awe and loyalty. He is the man who can relieve a tense deadlock in negotiations with a joke and start the talk on a new tack, as Jake Shafer did in William Foote Whyte's memorable case study, *Pattern of Industrial Peace*.[6] He is the man who faces a group that is weary, discouraged, depressed—and makes its members

---

6. William Foote Whyte, *Pattern of Industrial Peace* (New York: Harper & Brothers, 1951), pp. 70 ff., 180.

hold their sides with laughter. He is the man who can so effectively create cheer that no one dreams he has a toothache and would rather be killing a bottle of Scotch in a back room somewhere. He is also the man who steps between two quarreling people and gently urges them to reopen their minds. And he is the man who can be caught looking worried when everyone else is riding high or who can stir his people out of lethargy one day as he calmed them from panic a week before.

DELIBERATE STRENGTHENING OF DIFFERENCES

Despite circumstances that make individuality a natural outgrowth of management responsibility, the administrator may not be content to sit back. In order to "force" the development of differences, he may favor certain approaches.

Training by case method. The increasing popularity of the case method in company training programs, university's "advanced management" courses for executives, and business schools is generally attributed to the help the method offers in developing decision-making skills. There is also another reason. In discussing the action he would take on a specific case, the participant has an unusual chance to test and compare his values and assumptions with those held by others. He may object to the kind of long-range planning that other conferees support, for example, and he may suddenly realize that the real reason for his objection is not technical but an instinctive fear that large-scale planning will cramp initiative and freedom. Or he may be debating whether or not to fire a certain worker, when he suddenly sees that the real difference between the opposing views has little to do with the worker's record and ability but with built-in prejudices about "soreheads" or "trouble-makers." Or, in discussing a case on selling, he may see that, beneath the different points of view are different feelings about how aggressive a salesman should be.

The case discussion technique can be of inestimable value in bringing out such self-awareness and in sharpening one's sense of identity.

Objective analytical methods. A striking feature of many management techniques described in professional journals all over the world is the way in which problems are broken down into parts in the course of applying new approaches. For instance, methods of analyzing return on investment call for classifications of kinds of purpose, expense, income, and so forth. Methods of evaluating the desirability of manufacturing a new product call for splitting up the main question into series of sub-questions on such subjects as quality-price relationships, merchandisability, stability, breadth of market, and growth potential.

When using such methods, administrators are forced to spell out their reasoning and assumptions in some detail. They do not confront one another with sweeping final judgments. They meet instead along a broader front, with their differences and agreements spread over more territory than is the case with cruder methods. This complexity makes it more likely that a manager will develop more original thinking—not only because he must look more deeply into himself to reach a conclusion, but also because others are more inclined to expect and accept differences as thinking becomes more profound.

Differences among employees are commonly described as a problem or obstacle by writers on administration. "The manager often experiences his most uncomfortable moments when he has to deal with differences among people," say two business-school professors.[7] Young managers are advised by their seniors not to treat people uniformly, as if they were interchangeable machine parts, but to deal with each person individually. It is pointed out that, although this task is difficult, it must done.

The managerial mind does not deny this problem. But differences are also viewed as sources of strength—as perhaps the

7. Warren H. Schmidt and Robert Tannenbaum, "Management of Differences," *Harvard Business Review*, November-December, 1960, p. 107.

most under-rated asset in the literature of administration. Without them, creative relationships would be impossible. The recognition, appreciation, and encouragement of individuality is therefore important for not one but two reasons, for the sake of the
manager's personal effectiveness in getting work done through
others as well as for organizational effectiveness. Dealing with
differences is not simply a matter of technique but also of value,
and in terms of value it affects the manager's relationship to his
department or agency, as well as to his subordinate employees.

In a study of one effective pattern of operations in The Office
of The Assistant Secretary of the Air Force, John Glover and
Paul Lawrence noticed that a superior was often described in
this way: "You could always talk back to him if you wanted to"
or "You can always tell him what you think even if he doesn't
agree with you." [8] (In another, less effective pattern of operations, precisely the opposite type of remark was common.) Such
remarks are characteristically made in the kind of atmosphere
that, as I have tried to demonstrate, is associated with the administrative point of view. In this view, the best men are not
those who are most often on the side of the majority. The best
organizations are not those with the most perfect agreement
among people. Conformity may be a strong temptation, as de-
scriptions of "organization men" have shown, but it is only a
temptation. As a principle, it is inconsistent with the basic assumptions of management thinking.

IMPLICATIONS FOR INDIVIDUALS

For students, new managers, and veteran managers seeking to
formulate a philosophy of management, what are the implications of recognizing the value in differences?

---

8.   John D. Glover and Paul R. Lawrence, *A Case Study of High Level
Administration in a Large Organization* (Boston: Division of Research,
Harvard Business School, 1960), p. 68.

1. *There is a premium on knowledge—useful knowledge—of the way individuals act in groups and of the way groups act in relation to one another.* If managers regarded people simply as interchangeable factors (as some economists seem to do), such knowledge would not be unnecessary.

2. *The administrative philosophy is essentially liberal and democratic.* Despite the organizational necessity for command, direction, and obedience to authority, individuality demands the same abiding respect that it demands in progressive philosophies of education. In essence, the administrative point of view is not authoritarian or mechanistic, nor is it cynical about human nature.

3. *The management function is characterized by complexity and unceasing variety.* Managers should refute the impression frequently given in speeches and papers that good administration is a fairly cut-and-dried business. Rather, effective administration has mysterious depths and, after a point, seems beyond our present understanding. For many generations to come, there can be no new knowledge of group dynamics and personal relationships that will not be important to thoughtful managers. Administration itself should long continue to be one of the most fertile areas of research for social scientists.

4. *There are important differences between external and internal aspects of administration and between superficial appearances and realities.* Too often the public assumes that, because managers dress alike, for example, they also conform in their thinking or that, because an organization insists on certain procedures for dealers' advertising, it wants its employees and representatives to think alike, as well.

5. *The would-be manager must be prepared not only to "know his own mind" and its peculiarities but also to work for his ideas and "sell" them up and down the line.* He must also be prepared to stand alone in his views, for, as we have seen, the higher he goes in management, the more varied the circumstances

that will mold his thinking and make it different from that of other men. He will find it hard to be popular in the usual sense.

6. *There is no inherent reason that there should be less individuality and job challenge in large organizations than in small.* This statement flies in the face of an old and popular belief: that if you want to grow as an individual and "run with the ball" your chances are better in a small organization than in a giant one. It is reasoned that the smaller organization is less rigid, less bureaucratized, less restricted by rules and regulations. Overlooked, however, is the fact that the smaller firm or agency can also be a more tightly controlled one-man show; it is more easily dominated by an autocrat. More important is the influence of the managerial mind. If, as is often the case, its values and attitudes are influential in the administration of a large firm, there are unsurpassed opportunities for up-coming managers to develop an individual style. The large company, particularly if decentralized, offers a range and variety of challenge that is hard for the small firm to match. Both kinds of company can and do attract men with managerial minds.

4

TENSIONS

AND

THE

MANAGERIAL

ENVIRONMENT

IN THE MANAGERIAL MIND, the value of tension is closely related to the value of differences. Tension would not exist without differences, and it, in turn, makes differences more meaningful.

Tension does not have the same connotations for the administrator as for most other groups. It is not pejorative and does not signal breakdown or failure. Similarly, the opposite of tension —harmony, serenity, equilibrium—does not represent an ideal. The administrator rejects the notion that tension should be avoided if at all possible. He views tranquillity in an organization with alarm, associating it with sick enterprises and vulnerable departments. He finds tension not only acceptable but desirable. While setting limits on the desirable amount and drawing a distinction between tension and chaos, between stress and distress, he seeks to use tension in a positive way for the benefit of his organization.

Why Tension Is Valued

Why does the manager value tension? In answer, I draw first on an analogy made not by a manager but by a minister, Duncan E. Littlefair. His reasoning best sums up, for me, the feelings that a good many executives have expressed.

A sailboat makes its way because of the opposition of its sail to the wind. If this opposition is firm enough, the sailboat makes good progress, even against the wind. But if there is too much opposition between wind and sail, the boat may turn over, and if there is too little opposition, no headway is made. The setting of the sail against the wind must be done with judgment. This kind of opposition is vital in human relationships, Littlefair argues, and handling it with judgment is equally important.

So it is in administration. Men and women in the organization must oppose one another if they are to gain from association. If there is too little opposition, the relationships are static. If there is too much, the organization may be swamped. The amount of opposition, contradiction, attack, and defense must be firmly but reasonably controlled. A valuable relationship between two employees is one in which they stand against each other, without either seeking to ignore their opposition or putting it ahead of their working goals. Each profits from the other by being in motion against the other—by asserting different interests and contradictory views.

The kind of opposition to which I refer comes from healthy skepticism, genuine differences of opinion, and pursuit of one's self-interest. It is not the kind that results from malicious design, breakdowns in communication, stupidity, and obstructions of that nature.

What troubles the administrator about a tensionless organization is not the absence of conflict—because of course he knows that conflict exists in any group—but the refusal to admit and accept conflict, for then those involved never learn to take advantage of one another's individuality. When feelings finally do burst out of control, someone must resign or be fired.

"Creativity," "personal development," "productive interaction"—these words refer to a process that can be present only with tension. "Nothing comes from nothing," as King Lear said. Peter Drucker has pointed out that the developmental process is one that can occur only with "human resources." With non-human resources, output can never exceed input. "On the contrary, the problem in putting nonhuman resources together is always to keep to a minimum the inevitable output shrinkage through friction, etc. Man alone of all the resources available to man can grow and develop." [1]

The second reason for valuing tension is more personal: Tension is a condition for enjoyment of administrative work. The manager finds, as we all find, that there is no thrill of accomplishment without struggle, no release without a problem from which to be released, no elation without trial. A considerable amount of daily striving and self-assertion is necessary in the web of managerial relationships, else the administrative task becomes insufferably dull. A top-notch manager is likely to be a man who tells you that he gets a "bang out of his job." He has to risk a bang in the head to get it.

Sources and Applications

What are the possibilities for using tension to strengthen the organization? Let us turn now to important sources of tension and see how they relate to the manager's values.

---

1. Peter Drucker, *The Practice of Management* (New York: Harper & Brothers, 1954), p. 12.

Conflicting interests. Tension can arise from conflicts of interest. One illustration is that of an oil-equipment firm, in which management was divided into two camps over the question of how much emphasis to put on new products. The following excerpt comes from an argument made one day by the works manager, a man identified in the case (names were disguised) as Fred Schmidt. He was debating company policy in a group that included Bill Ellsworth, the vice-president and advertising manager.

The only thing I want to put across is this. I'm not against making new stuff, not at all, but I want you—I want everybody—to realize you're at the point where you cannot go very much farther with new stuff and keep up the old at the same time, because we're limited in space. That's all there is to it. Now if the thing to do is to expand, well, O.K., let's expand, but we have to go into it with open eyes, and I think Bill's idea of—well, you're creating manufacturing problems constantly and I'm going to try to create sales problems making the things we have, and it's just a tossup between the two of us. That's what I'm after. I'm going to try to make you fellows produce more, and sell more in the lines we have. That's how we make our money. We don't make it if we have to develop something new all the time. Have you ever realized how many dies we have down there?—punch-press dies—we have a measly little punch press. We have two now, but I mean one is in operation, and I think we have 450 or 500 punch-press dies down there! Every time you bring in a new product, that means new dies, and I'm beginning not to know where to put them any more! For such small items our drill jigs are the same thing! We've got hundreds of them! We have hundreds of thousands of dollars tied up in drills, and in jigs, and in tools and equipment of that kind, and every time you make a little change and bring something new out it's a big investment! We have to get the money to make those things! That's the only thing I'm after! There's no other way out of it! Well, O.K., we'll make something new every day. That's all right, but you want to do it with open eyes. You want to know what we're doing. . . . [2]

---

2. Wilton Oil Equipment Company (B), Harvard Business School case. Copyright by the President and Fellows of Harvard College.

Here is a natural and common type of conflict of interest: a production man who wants to put the brakes on product innovation for the sake of costs and quality pitted against a marketing man who wants a steady stream of new products for the sake of sales.

What value does the manager see in this form of tension? He sees that each of the men—in this case, Schmidt and Ellsworth—is working in his own way for what he considers to be the best interests of the company. Each man is sufficiently interested in the company so that he is willing to stand up and argue for what he thinks right. Clearly, such enthusiasm is precious to the organization, and by having the conflict in the open—in everyday discussion—the managers have a better chance to learn from it, to absorb other men's information and reasoning. Equally important, they are better able to keep the conflict within reasonable bounds so that it does not get too big to handle. Both Schmidt and Ellsworth will develop more rapidly as individuals if they can relish the tension between them, and the company will profit from a wiser synthesis of sales and production thinking.

Keeping up with change. A second source of tension is change in the environment. If a federal regulatory agency could count on the same violations at the same rate, unchanging public opinion, and constant ages and capabilities of its staff members, then management might hope some day to perfect its policies and procedures—if it worked very hard. Once they were perfected, management would not have to worry about them any more. In reality, however, as we all know, the nature and pace of violations is constantly changing, and so are public opinion, the ages and capabilities of staff members, and many other factors. Consequently, the policies and procedures of the agency are forever out of date, no matter how hard managers work at improving them. No sooner are revisions made than the circumstances that prompted them change, so that new action is again needed. Both conscious and subconscious awareness of this problem causes tension.

In marketing, to take another example, much the same is true. One corporate executive has stated that "There is probably no marketing plan in industry today that is not out-of-date. . . . The reason is that there are so many constantly changing factors in any company's marketing situation that it is practically impossible to keep revising a plan so rapidly and so accurately that there is no lag in it." [3]

Why does this kind of tension have a value in the managerial mind? It can serve as a kind of bridge to more inquiry and interaction among people in the organization. The fact that they worry about change and are not sure how best to deal with it is an incentive to thinking, learning, and teamwork. I know of one top management group that, prompted by strong industry competition and changing markets, decided to sit down regularly with department and division heads to review the profit objectives set for the forthcoming year. Were the targets high enough? Were the programs for reaching them sound? This give-and-take between headquarters and divisional heads soon became valuable not only in planning but in strengthening the entire management set-up. The need for it would not have been recognized but for tension.

Some business leaders have been notable for never letting their organizations forget to worry about uncertainty. A shrewd *Fortune* reporter once made the following observation about Harlow Curtice during his heyday as president of General Motors Corporation:

Harlow Curtice is permanently and violently at war with complacency, and in effect runs his powerhouse of a company with all the urgency of some desperately worried, embattled executive who isn't sure where his next dollar is coming from, whose competitors are breathing fire in his face, and who is in imminent danger, at the slightest slackening or oversight, of seeing his customers desert him in droves. . . . By the force of his own example, Curtice has his team running scared. That the need for its doing so is a slight

3. Arthur P. Felton, "Conditions of Marketing Leadership," *Harvard Business Review*, March-April, 1956, p. 119.

exaggeration of the facts of life is revealed by a popular family joke around G.M. Whenever the company's 51 per cent share of the industry's volume is mentioned, someone is sure to say, "You know what the boss says—it means we're losing almost five out of every ten deals."[4]

Differing perceptions. A common cause of tension within the individual is differences between what he sees to be true and what he thinks should be true or should be done to change the situation. If the gap becomes too large, when he loses touch with reality or aspires to do too much, a breakdown results. Similarly, a major source of tension within the organization is differing perceptions about the nature of problems and what action should be taken. Note that these variations are due not only to contrasting backgrounds and interests but also to differences in the order of events as seen or described, differences in the amount of information received, and so forth. A knowledgeable college dean has commented on what may seem to be perversities of behavior that result:

. . . a worker may perceive an offer of increased authority as a dangerous removal from the safety of assured, though gradual, promotion. A change in channels of authority or reporting, no matter how valuable in increasing efficiency, may be thought of as a personal challenge or affront. The introduction of a labor-saving process may be perceived as a threat to one's job. An invitation to discuss company policy may be perceived as an elaborate trap to entice one into admitting heretical or disloyal views. A new fringe benefit may be regarded as an excuse not to pay higher salaries.[5]

What use does this sort of tension have? It has a creative value. A man's imagination may start working when someone else, looking at the identical situation he is studying, describes it differently. Also, divergent opinions may provide the irritation needed to keep his thinking going. As many an artist is indebted to critics who have trained themselves to be cruelly frank rather

---

4. The Editors of Fortune, *The Art of Success* (New York: J. B. Lippincott Company, 1956), pp. 6, 8.

5. W. C. H. Prentice, "Understanding Leadership," *Harvard Business Review,* September-October, 1961, p. 145.

than polite in their reactions, so many organizational workers are spurred to creative work by the criticism of associates who do not agree with them. Chris Argyris reports an extreme example in a plant he studied. One of the supervisors commented on the manager as follows:

> I told him once that I didn't know how the hell to please him and he told me, "Look here, I'm not going to let you alone. I'm not ever going to let you alone. If you ever get to a point where you think you know your job too well, then you become like a stagnant pool. I'm going to keep after you all the time." [6]

Differing perceptions are useful only within a certain range, however, for if the irritations and conflicts they create get out of hand, what might have been a value quickly becomes a "disvalue." Accordingly, the good manager is likely to watch this form of tension with special care lest too *much* wind get in the sails. See how firmly the supervisor intervenes in the following incident, which is taken from a case report on a human-relations crisis in a nuclear-tube assembly room (the workers' argument is over the responsibility for some leaky stems in the product):

> I had asked everybody to get together in my office for a talk. When we all got together in here, I told them that I understood how it was they were feeling, how everyone had gotten so tense and nervous over those stems, that everybody was ready to blow her lid. Then I said, "It has spread to the rest of the department, too. Every girl in the room is involved and the whole department is suffering. Now," I said, "let's face it, you're acting like a bunch of children. You're not children; you're grown, mature women, and isn't it time you stopped all this and started to build up your relations with one another, your cooperative, friendly spirit that is so important to the department's success." I had led up to this slowly, giving them every impression that I understood what their feelings were, not denying them, but telling them also that it was time to stop whatever had been going on and to do something about it. Then, I sat back and let it explode, and boy, did it, all over the place. That's just what I wanted so I let them go at it tooth and nail. There were feelings being spilled in every direction.

6. Chris Argyris, *Executive Leadership* (New York: Harper & Brothers. 1953), p. 82.

I know they all said things they were going to regret later but it had to happen that way. When I thought it had gone on long enough, I said, "Okay, hold it just a minute. I would like to make a suggestion." I then outlined a proposition . . . I told them whatever the outcome, it didn't matter to me but that this would be for their benefit, to find out something. I didn't get a big response to this so I let it go. Feelings were still running pretty high so I let it rage on again for awhile and then told them in no uncertain terms that this was going to have to stop.[7]

The tendency to dissent. A fourth source of tension develops because of advance planning. When decisions are made respecting the direction of future growth and change, not all employees can be expected to agree with every point, yet the general weight of opinion can make the dissenter's life difficult.

The leaders in advance planning recognize this danger and make an effort to prevent it by keeping plans flexible. Yet the mere fact that an organization plans means that it becomes committed. Suppose that a company sets a sales goal—a sound and well-defined goal, let us hope, and an ambitious one. Now, a carefully thought-out goal requires much research and analysis, many conferences, considerable soul-searching. To revise the goal is therefore also likely to require considerable trial and effort, especially in the absence of dramatic errors that make the need for change obvious. Does not the very act of commitment—the fact that the sales organization has already made up its mind— carry with it the possibility that suggested departures will meet a cold reaction? "We went all through that last year," people will moan when a man comes up with a new planning idea, "and it was hard enough then. Why does he have to rock the boat?"

In short, the very existence of an agreed-upon plan tends to make a nonconforming opinion more noticeable—and a source of tension. Without the plan, the conflict in opinion might not be nearly so apparent. Managers would not have clear benchmarks for assessing the differences.

---

7. American Radiatronics Corporation (B), a Harvard Business School case. Copyright 1960 by the President and Fellows of Harvard College.

What value does this type of tension have? It tends to keep members of management more critical of the planning process. If there is confusion about a plan, how did it happen? Is the program out of date? Should certain assumptions in it be changed? Discerning thought about questions like these may well spell much of the difference between successful and unsuccessful planning in industry today.

Competition vs. co-operation. In our national economic policy, we stress the role of competition among organizations. The rivalry between Macy's and Gimbels, Ford and Chevrolet dealers and countless others is a part of our culture. Within organizations, we also agree that a certain amount of competitiveness is good. It may be frankly encouraged by compensation, promotion, and job-assignment policies. Much of the emphasis here is on teamwork and cooperation, however. We offer a worker incentives to make a better record than anyone else, but at the same time we expect him to co-operate in getting certain jobs done. These often inconsistent expectations lead to another form of tension in employee groups.

For example, debates over intra-company pricing policy have reportedly led to executive fist-fights in industry. Suppose that a corporation has two separately organized and operated divisions, A and B. A makes clocks, and B makes certain parts used in clocks. A can obtain this part from an outside supplier for a slightly lower price than it can from B. If, therefore, A wants to make the best possible profit record, it will buy from the outside supplier—and certainly many corporate policies endorse such actions. Suppose, however, that B is operating at half capacity. Every idle machine and worker in the B plant cost B *and* the parent company money. If A buys from B, A's profit will be slightly lower, but the profit of the corporation as a whole will be better. What should A do? There is no easy answer, especially if we are judging the showing of A's managers by comparison with the showing of other division managers.

This type of tension also has its uses. The conflict between competition and cooperation serves as a continual reminder that both are important and should be preserved. The question is what kind of balance to strike. Business, educational, and government undertakings are governed by complex value systems affecting this question. These systems change continually with usage over the years, as the law changes with usage. The standards applied tomorrow will be different from the ones applied today, as those today are different from those of decades ago. Standards also vary from organization to organization. (The divisional pricing problem just described is an excellent case in point, as practices in the oil and automobile industries demonstrate.) The problem is to see that these changes reflect conscious management goals, rather than mere happenstance. It is at this point that tension helps, because it supplies the necessary motive and interest for open discussion of the problems that managers face in trying to meet the conflicting requirements of competition and cooperation.

The challenge of leadership. Most men and women improve their skills as administrators and leaders only with considerable effort. They must acquire new knowledge, learn new ways of thinking, and perhaps even change their styles of living. Such shifts create tension in the mind of the person who is trying to make them and in his relationship with others. This stress, according to some specialists in management training, is sufficient to keep some men from advancing far.

What value does such tension have in the managerial mind? First, it is a good screening device. If an ambitious manager can't live with the tension of self-reorientation, he is not likely to withstand the stress of a higher office. Second and more important, such tension is a condition of development. The manager must experience the conflict between old and new concepts before he can purposefully take steps toward a necessary change.

Here again, however, tension is valuable only within limits, and assessing those limits properly is a critical task for the executive in charge. A particularly good example is supervisory development in advanced-technology industries where work is done on a task-force or project basis. Here the supervisor is likely to be an engineer making the exceedingly difficult transition from being "technically oriented" to being "management oriented." The stress of such a jump must be neither too great nor too small, as a project manager at Westinghouse Electric Corporation has testified:

> The first-line supervisors—the "supervising engineers"—are by definition the men who play the key roles in guiding the day-by-day progress of a project toward its goals. Such a supervisor often bears the same range of burdens borne by his manufacturing counterpart; demands on his time can easily be overpowering if the project manager does not act to shield him from diversionary requirements.
>
> At the same time it should be borne in mind that in attempting to shield a supervisor, to free him to concentrate chiefly on the vital engineering job at hand, the project manager can unknowingly deal a severe blow to the supervisor's advancement potential. The supervisor is at a critical point in his career, at which leadership capability and administrative potential can blossom or be blighted. A general and basic tenet of management—the training of individuals for leadership—must not be shelved merely because the pace of an advanced-technology project seems at times to be overpowering. Instead the project manager must walk the middle course. For example, he may shield the supervisor from poorly founded requests for detailed information by a staff office, while at the same time letting him resolve with the personnel department a tough question in personnel administration involving one of his engineers.[8]

Without the experience of challenging negotiations with the personnel department, the supervisor may miss the opposition he needs to develop his ability, but with it *and* other demands too, he may find himself swamped.

In sum, at least six kinds of tension have value in the administrative scheme. Tension resulting from conflicting interests is a sign of concern and increases opportunities for learning. Ten-

---

8. Paul O. Gaddis, "The Project Manager," *Harvard Business Review*, May-June, 1959, p. 92.

sion resulting from change in the environment is an incentive to inquiry and teamwork. Stress arising from differing perceptions may stimulate creativity. Certain tensions imposed by planning provide a basis for alternative plans. The conflict between demands for co-operation and competition is a reminder of the importance of each to the organization. And the strain of adjusting to new responsibilities has a role in the process of self-development.

Of course, most sources of tension are useful only up to a point. What was once a value can become a "disvalue" if carried too far. At some point or series of points, stress becomes distress. Also, not all kinds of tension are desirable. For instance, managers will not value tensions resulting from dishonesty, the behavior of emotionally disturbed personalities, or the frustration of a group that lacks, because of misdirection, the proper amount of authority to do its job.

All this suggests that tension is a good example of the importance of values in describing the managerial mind and of the unimportance of techniques of action. For while a particular value is universally important in the minds of men responsible for productive group effort, or so I maintain, the kind of administrative action that is considered desirable varies radically from situation to situation. For example, the capacity of people to tolerate tension depends heavily on whether or not they feel a sense of mission about the organization and believe deeply in its importance. The more they share this sense, the more support they find in working together, and the more differences they can accept. An administrator's convictions about what is and what is not effective supervision are only likely, therefore, to reflect the sense of mission that he sees in the organization. They have no significance whatever—to him or to others—in another situation where the tolerance for tension is at a different level.

Accordingly, while most of the "do's" and "don'ts" regarding the handling of employee disputes, friction, composition of work groups, and so forth may be useful indeed as suggestions, they do not offer distinguishing characteristics of the administrator's point of view. It is the initial assumption he makes about tension that sets him apart from the nonmanager and identifies his approach when he is given management responsibility.

IMPLICATIONS FOR INDIVIDUALS

What is the significance of this discussion for those trying to size up the quality of managerial thinking? Here are some points for the student, the professional man edging from staff work into administration, the young manager—and especially for those wondering if managing an organization calls only for the dog-eat-dog, self-promoting, wheeling-and-dealing type of outlook so often portrayed in popular literature.

1. *Probably every organization has some of the destructive tensions played up in fiction and satires, but they are only part of the story.* Wherever the self-promoters and power-grabbers thrive there must also be—or recently have been—managers working in a more productive way for the organization, else there could be no prize to try to grab off. An organization populated mainly by the management characters portrayed by Scott Fitzgerald, Theodore Dreiser, or John Dos Passos, and subject only to the kinds of tensions such men create, would soon be reduced to nothing. It is up to the individual to choose which camp he wants to join, which kind of tension he wants to create.

2. *To cope with administrative tension successfully, the individual must have a strong desire for self-development.* His answer to tension must not be to give in to it but to use it as a means of enlarging his understanding. While feeling committed to the organization, he does not subjugate himself to it. There is a big difference between the two kinds of response.

3. *Administration is not the only field where tension is valued.* For instance, the medical profession places a value on tension when it encourages group practice; teachers often value the

tensions created by class discussion; and so on. Note, too, that many philosophies and religions have by inference valued tension by teaching individual salvation through stress, discipline, self-subordination, and sacrifice of self-interest.

4. *The attitude toward tension is part of the explanation for the tremendous satisfactions many managers get from managerial life.* Managers are like golfers whose tension on the course culminates in the thrill of a fine game. Aspirants to management might well ask themselves whether they want this kind of pleasure from life, with all its peaks and valleys—like Theodore Roosevelt's doctrine of the strenuous life—or prefer a more level, more subdued flow of satisfaction.

5. *The attitude toward tension helps keep the personal element in management in high gear.* There are writers and speakers who mourn that management has become a morass of synthetic procedures, routines, and data, and the administrative mind distorted by the lack of real-life contacts. This view is not a balanced one, according to the standards described here. The importance attached to tension, along with other administrative values, keeps administration personal, first-hand, urgent, and full of give and take. It also means that there is a high premium on being able to maintain one's personal relationships in the face of strain and adversity, viz., not feeling that a relationship with a person must be cut off simply because of a disagreement with him or a conflict of interest. The head of a fast-growing, planning-conscious British electronics firm once commented on his actions at board meetings: "I usually endeavor to`bring out something controversial so that at least one member of the board will get hot under the collar about it. If we can each of us do this without fear then I think we are creating a very powerful team relationship." [9]

---

9. The Solartron Electronic Group Ltd. (A). Copyright 1959 by l'Institut pour l'Etude des Méthodes de Direction de l'Entreprise, Lausanne, Switzerland.

5

THE

MANAGERIAL

ZEST

FOR

PROBLEMS

IN 1926, GEORGE BORG, pioneer developer of the automobile clutch and the first president of Borg-Warner Corporation, said in a letter to his friend, Marshall Beck:

I have been following a homely philosophy that impressed me the moment I was able to have any understanding of this complicated world: that life is essentially the overcoming of obstacles, that one can—and must—get enjoyment out of the overcoming of obstacles. And I have found that it is a philosophy that works.[1]

---

1. Robert J. Casey, *Mr. Clutch* (New York: The Bobbs-Merrill Company, 1948), p. 174.

Possibly no aspect of the managerial mind is more baffling and frustrating to the nonmanager than this attitude toward problems and difficulties. It is an attitude characterized by a willingness to disturb, to probe, to "look for trouble," and even to "make trouble." He is like an engineer who is never satisfied with his work, however perfect it may seem to others, but is always tinkering with it, stopping the machine to see if he can find a trouble spot or a way of making it run better.

To the nonmanager this enthusiasm may seem pathological. Indeed, in many books and articles about administration written by nonadministrators, there is the frequently recurring assumption —conscious or unconscious—that problems are a necessary evil and a threat and that the fewer the administrator has to face, the luckier he is. That quite a contrary view is held by the man with a managerial mind is due in large part, again, to certain assumptions he makes about how an organization lives and grows.

The most important of these assumptions is that problems provide a springboard for men who seek change and improvement. Conversely, if the leaders of an organization avoid problems or refuse to recognize them, it will almost certainly decline. A military unit may cling to a procedure that is hopelessly out of date. A government bureau may persist stubbornly with a policy of promotion from within that should have been discarded years ago. A foundry may follow a fifty-year-old custom of refusing to go into debt for new equipment, even though times have changed and the risk of debt has become smaller than the risk of depending on obsolete equipment. A family concern may continue unquestioned a policy of nepotism that was originally justified—as at the Brown Company during the 1920's. "The Brown sons all went to college at Williams, all took the grand tour, and all returned to New Hampshire to run the company," it is reported. "All was ordered, and seemingly forever." [2] The company was a sitting duck for bankruptcy when the depression came along.

---

2. The Editors of Fortune, *The Art of Success* (New York: J. B. Lippincott Company, 1956), p. 46.

In short, the most dangerous problem an enterprise or agency can have, from a managerial point of view, is a *lack* of problems —or, more precisely, a failure to recognize problems. Organizations get into more trouble from the problems they don't face than from those they do face. A problem may not necessarily be solved successfully, but the challenge it offers will serve to test the muscles of the organization—to "exercise it." While this physical analogy should not be pressed too far, it is valid to a degree and sometimes helps managers to explain their point of view. For example,

The corporation is like a living organism. All of you gentlemen have watched with much fascination, I'm sure, the changes that have taken place in your own business organizations over a period of years. There seem to be recurrent cycles in which management power and influence flow in toward the center and then out to the extremities. Strange, hard-to-diagnose illnesses occur in various parts of the organism; unsightly bulges appear anywhere that fat is permitted to accumulate. . . .

If the organism is permitted to sit still too long, it begins to develop hardening of the arteries, shortness of breath, and atrophy of the imagination. The executive must be constantly and critically sensitive to the health of the corporate organization, and experimental, intuitive, and imaginative in dealing with it.[3]

COMMON BLINDERS

Presently I shall examine in more detail how the managerial mind reacts to administrative problems, but first let us put this topic in perspective. Members of organizations—including those who perform managerial tasks—have contrived a variety of techniques for avoiding problems. A brief review of these devices should help us to appreciate the significance of what the manager with George Borg's philosophy is trying to do.

---

3. Ernest R. Breech, "The Large Company: Basic Strategy," *Harvard Business School Bulletin,* Summer, 1955, pp. 26-29. The paper was originally delivered at the National Business Conference, Harvard Business School, in June, 1955.

Overemphasis on security. In governmental, industrial, educational, philanthropic, athletic, and other organizations, the members continuously seek to make their jobs and positions secure. Of course, there is a value in this effort. It fulfills a human need, and up to a point it stimulates competition. If it becomes a preoccupation, however, it becomes dangerous, for the condition of absolute security is necessarily the avoidance of risk and change.

Similarly, departments and divisions as a whole are forever seeking to gain protected positions. In one large company, for example, the top six or seven functional heads have built up little "empires." Within each empire, the head is a virtual czar. There is an informal understanding that the other vice presidents will not interfere with him or his subordinates. In its early stages, this empire-building might have been more beneficial than harmful. After all, executives need some kind of protection against arbitrary and impulsive interference from other men, and lightly-drawn boundaries are useful for this purpose. Efforts to ensure protection can be too successful, however. Today those empires have grown so strong that the company finds it difficult to engage in thoughtful questioning of basic departmental policies and goals. To the extent that the empires have become impregnable, it is now almost impossible to face up to the growing problems that must be dealt with effectively if the organization itself is to continue to grow.

Putting harmony first. Because so many natural sources of disagreement exist in the modern industrial or governmental organization, there is a constant temptation to retreat to some kind of "harmony house" where the notes of discord can no longer be heard. For instance, if operations researchers have been called in to solve a management problem, it is tempting to restrict their studies to "safe" areas and to rule out any discomfiting questions about important assumptions and policies. Again, in evaluating new investment projects, it is tempting to accept a particular return-on-investment formula "so we won't have any big arguments any more."

Up to a point, of course, efforts to avoid controversy and to assure "smooth sailing" serve a worthwhile purpose; people must get on with the day's work. But the effort to make a fetish of agreement must be listed as a second device for obscuring problems that exist.

Substituting routines for thinking. Some routines are necessary and helpful. They make it unnecessary to stop and think before every act, and they add consistency. But what if the manager comes to use routines *instead* of thinking? Suppose, for example, that he devises elaborate channels of communication to protect his privacy. He may give so much attention to procedure that he has little time for the content of his communications. He may succeed in protecting his privacy so well that the man with a suggestion must go through too many channels to reach him and may give up the whole idea—convenient for those whose routines might have been changed by the suggestion, perhaps, but not for the organization as a whole.

Routine has long been the despair of those who want management to venture more often into thinking about the uncertain future. Indeed, a kind of "Gresham's Law" has been attributed to routine. "Daily routine drives out planning," two writers claim. "Stated less cryptically, we predict that when an individual is faced both with highly programmed and unprogrammed tasks, the former tend to take precedence over the latter even in the absence of strong over-all time pressure." [4] It is when organizational behavior works in strong support of this tendency and threatens to make it rigid that a red flag is raised in the managerial mind.

"Schedulitis." Managers and supervisors typically have full and busy days. They run meetings that must be hurried because

---

4. James G. March and Herbert A. Simon, *Organizations* (New York: John Wiley & Sons, Inc., 1958), p. 185.

there is so much business to cover. They are responsible for the
work of a clerical force or production crew so large that they
can oversee only part of it personally and must select some sort
of control measure to judge output and performance. In one way
after another, they are under pressure to assign priorities and use
short cuts.

If the manager wants to shut the problems of change and
growth out of his mind, *if* he wants to let inertia take over, he has
easy excuses. To avoid seeing someone who disturbs him, he has
but to point to a full calendar. To avoid new ideas in conference,
he has but to force the meeting through the agenda fast enough so
that only perfunctory comments can be made—a never-ending
temptation that he needs help in resisting. Much depends on
whether or not the general mood and atmosphere of the organization will support him.

Compulsion to show status. In the office of one radio-station
executive, I am told, there is a pitcher of water on a tray with
one glass. In the office of his senior, there is a water pitcher with
two glasses, and in the office of that man's senior, a water pitcher
with three glasses. Status symbols of this kind are, of course,
legendary in business and government. The size of the office will
be carefully determined by the height of an executive's position,
officers will be separated from "the men" by having a special
bathroom down the hall, and so forth.

Showing status is such a normal human tendency that no
one will quarrel with it up to a point. It is when it becomes a
preoccupation, and particularly when it becomes a substitute for
inquiry and argument, that the manager objects. For it is then
that the man with three water glasses is tempted to save himself
the bother of argument with the man with only two glasses, on
grounds of higher status, rather than relying on superior reasoning. The man who has been promoted to an office on the same
floor as the president's may use his power to avoid concerning

himself with the unpleasantness of customer complaints, rather than organizing better ways of handling the criticisms.

Preoccupation with orderliness. If members of a group want badly to avoid the mess and confusion of change, they can be "reasonable" about it. In order to avoid being disturbed, they can simply aspire to very modest goals. In order to spare themselves hurt feelings and failure, they can make it a point not to do anything unconventional. They can make neatness and tranquillity their objectives, and they can see that nothing upsets their pet schemes and prejudices.

This attitude is a subtle one, but it can be communicated. One executive makes routine visits among workers asking, "Is everything all right?" The manner of his asking makes it plain that he expects "Yes" or "Okay" for an answer, and those are the answers he gets. It is plain to everyone that any other answer will upset his scheme of things. Another executive who makes the same kind of visit and asks the same question may get the same answer, but he follows it up. "How about the lighting over there, is that all right?" "What about that mess in order pick-ups last week, what was the story behind that?" It begins to be apparent that he is looking for realities, that he *really* wants to know. Better information will soon be coming to him, with all that it means for possibilities of progress.

Obsession with firm conclusions. People who feel insecure in the face of problems and are worried at the implications of change are frequently tempted to spare themselves from unpleasantness by coming to quick conclusions. The man who bangs his fist down early in the argument and says, "I believe in taking a firm stand," is likely to be the one who can't stand the uncertainty of questions and new ideas. He is the man to whom everything must be either right or wrong. The public relations program is good, or it is bad. Motivation research is useful, or it is nonsense. The Democrats are progressive, or they are all bums. The treasurer is a sound man or a fraud. And so forth.

Such black and white reasoning, needless to say, interferes greatly with recognition of problems. It is in the gray areas that the big problems develop, and a good deal of probing is necessary to see what is happening.

The Pattern of Tough-Mindedness

Given these common techniques for avoiding problems—and surely one could add many more to this short list—how does the manager resist them? More precisely, what particular points of view does he demonstrate in the effort to focus more rather than less attention on problems and to add zest and interest, rather than fear and indifference, to the challenge of facing them? These questions help to explain an attitude sometimes described as "tough-mindedness"—the willingness, when necessary, to take the unpopular step when others hesitate to stir things up or probe tender spots. "Tough-mindedness" refers to a set of attitudes and assumptions that makes attacking problems seem natural, necessary, and rewarding.

The realization that creative relationships may be difficult and harsh. This attitude is directly opposed to the school of thought that the most perfect relationship is the smoothest and most loving one. The manager's attitude, in effect, is that it would be nice to have complete security. It would be nice to have harmonious meetings. It would be comfortable to stick to schedules and routines. The desire for status is understandable. It would be wonderful always to have order instead of confusion. But effective management puts growth and creativity first, and change, uncertainty, and upset are necessary conditions for growth and creativity. To be productive means sometimes, at least, to be very tough.

When these attitudes are translated into action, it is only natural that the manager is often resented. A man does not upset comfortable routines or introduce problems without creating antipathy, even among those who recognize and understand the importance of his general purposes. His choice is never completely right. When, exactly, does a routine become too comfortable? When does the quest for security go too far? Such questions are never clear-cut. The administrator must willingly accept the consequences of cutting through the jungle of dissenting opinions. Here is a revealing episode from the life of P. W. Litchfield, a founder and head of Goodyear Tire & Rubber Company:

An emergency arose one night. The rubberized fabric as it comes from the calendars is cut to size and stored in wooden racks until needed. That night one rack, overloaded, gave way and fell against the adjoining one, which yielded with the impact and soon all of them were tumbling down like a house of cards. Two days' production was a mass of wood, nails, rubber, fabric. The factory would have to close down shortly for lack of stock unless something was done.

Slusser [a young vice-president] went into action. Picking men from other departments, he put everyone to work there was room for, to calender new fabric, set carpenters to making new racks, had a third group cleaning up the debris.

Anyone would call this initiative, recognizing an emergency, and doing something about it, fast. The youngster from the coal mines, to whom Stephens had given his trust, was trying to meet it and was doing an excellent job.

But Bill State [the chief engineer] heard about it, left dinner to hurry out to the plant, took over, began to issue orders. Slusser challenged him and the battle was on.

"Steve left me in charge," was Slusser's final argument. "I've told the men what to do."

"You're not telling my men what to do," said State. "They don't work for you. I am sending them back to their jobs. And you're going to hear from this."

He was in my office the next morning pounding on the desk.

"This place isn't big enough for Slusser and me both," he said. "You'll have to get rid of him or I'm quitting."

Which was something of a problem for the superintendent. State's gifts in engineering and machine design in a struggling business, his dynamic energy in the erection of buildings and procurement of machines made him practically indispensable. On the other hand, I felt that Cliff [Slusser] was one of the most promising young men I had known. But he was wrong in this case—and it was not the first time he had had trouble with other departments. This was something I had to straighten out. These things are not pleasant, but when a man is doing something wrong, you are doing him no favor by not telling him so. Even vice presidents have to be called on the carpet occasionally.

I took most of the steam out of State's complaint by agreeing with him. Slusser had far exceeded his authority.

"I'll handle it, Bill," I said. "Go on back and forget about it."

Then I called Cliff in and tried to point out some of the practical facts of business in a large organization, perhaps in a little different way than they were set down in the Alexander Hamilton course.

"You've done good work here and should go far," I said, "but one thing stands in your way. A business like ours is made up of many departments, and it is my job to co-ordinate them, see that they work together smoothly, act as a team. When you take an assignment, you don't seem to realize that other departments have problems, and lines of authority, you go roughshod over anybody who gets in your way. I don't know whether you realize it or not, but you've made bad friends for yourself all over the plant. In an organization such as this we're trying to carry on, you've made it impossible for me to promote you to a better job."

Slusser, barely twenty at the time, just sat there looking at me I felt sorry for him, but this was a surgical operation and surgeons cannot be kind. I had to make this stick in his mind.

"Cliff," I finished, "you can expect a promotion only when a job is open and these other men come in and tell me you're the man to take it. It's all up to you." [5]

What Mr. Litchfield was doing in this case is a hard thing to do. It takes strong motivations to be able to do it, as well as a particular aptitude. A man must be determined to make a lot of money, or he must be under terrific pressure to meet some kind of goal—or he must be a manager.

In this instance, I think it is clear that Mr. Litchfield was thinking of his organization. He and Slusser were both working

---

5. From *The Industrial Voyage*, by P. W. Litchfield. Copyright 1954 by P. W. Litchfield. Reprinted by permission of Doubleday & Company, Inc.

for the success of the plant. They had that goal in common, and it kept them striving in the same direction despite different temperaments, backgrounds, and responsibilities. To make their relationship a productive one, however, the boss had to be blunt and tough.

Recognition that a certain amount of failure should be valued. This recognition does not mean that failure no longer hurts; it does. What it means is that failures are indispensable in uncovering strengths and weaknesses and that, in the long run, knowledge of these strengths and weaknesses can be turned to greater advantage by the manager than can a perfect record.

A perfect record can, in fact, be exceedingly dangerous. First, it leads to complacency. So long as nothing goes wrong, discerning questions are not likely to be raised, and there is a strong temptation to equate what the organization is currently doing with what it should always be doing. For example, if it is making a certain type of automobile, training with a certain kind of weapon, or educating students in a certain way, the tendency is to accept this performance as the standard for success and security. With such a narrow "self-concept," the organization is at a paralyzing disadvantage when conditions change and new kinds of transportation, warfare, or education are needed. The danger of continuous success, in other words, is that it tempts employees to forget that their real strength, in the last analysis, is their ability to respond through creative interaction to the ever-changing needs of the world they serve.

There is a second and more important reason for fearing too smooth a record of success. The manager senses that no organization can have such a record if it is raising its sights high enough. Lack of failure is a sign of lack of aggressiveness. Unless he can somehow coax his department or enterprise to reach for a little more than it can surely grasp and can deliberately drive it to taste frustration from time to time, he can never claim that he has done his utmost to help it learn and progress. He does not fear "pushing the luck" of an organization too far, "asking for too much" from a work group, or forcing a conflict into the open, simply because trouble and failure may result (although he must, of course, see a positive value to be gained).

This insight is an old one, and it has been meaningful to many peoples in many different kinds of situations. In India, for example, where productivity has taken on such crucial importance, the head of a tobacco factory has commented:

It is . . . the duty of the senior manager to influence his men and to encourage them to think about the job and to help them to formulate and crystallize their ideas. He has to keep an objective before his men which is ever-receding. If one objective is achieved, another should be placed before them. This requires foresight, keeping in mind possibilities which recede, and realising these possibilities at the right time under the right conditions.

The importance of an ever-receding objective cannot be exaggerated; but if the senior man places one objective in front of his men and that objective is achieved and he has not got another objective to place before them, thinking stops at the different levels, complacency sets in and the desirable upward movement of the graph to increase productivity begins to taper off. Once creative thinking stops and the upward graph tends to level off, it is indeed an extremely difficult task for the same manager to push it up again. It requires double the effort to restart creative thinking once again at all levels.[6]

Determination to keep the organization restless, discontented, flexible, and not too confident. How can men be kept from specializing too much? How can they be prevented from settling on fixed goals and shutting out other possibilities? What can be done to ensure that a department or division will not develop rigid routines? The manager makes it his business to worry about such questions. He is therefore continually in danger of stirring up more trouble than his goal is worth, of trying to "play God," of intruding more than is necessary. Instinct and experience tell him that it is necessary to run these risks, however, for otherwise

---

6. B. K. Nehru, "Top Management and Productivity," *Applied Economic Papers* (Department of Commerce, Osmania University, Hyderabad, India), March, 1961, p. 23.

his organization will almost certainly suffer from "hardening of the policies." The graveyard of governmental, business, and other organizations is full of those that died from it.

When Clarence Randall was head of Inland Steel, for example, he was likely to take a young man settling into a comfortable production job, yank him from the routine, and give him a tough assignment in sales. Some executives in education and government go to great pains to keep certain men, consultants, or committees at work questioning the objectives and procedures of different departments. The so-called marketing concept has also become a powerful device, in the hands of some managers, for keeping minds open about the basic products and services that the firm should be trying to sell. The motive force is the haunting fear of becoming committed to an outmoded or unprofitable product or industry. In the words of Saki's verse,

> Some laud a life of mild content:
> Content may fall, as well as Pride.
> The Frog who hugged his lowly Ditch
> Was much disgruntled when it dried.[7]

Still another suggestion for dealing with "hardening of the policies" has been put forth by Murray D. Lincoln, the well-known co-operative leader:

Any organization, once it becomes successful, is apt to lose its original drive and vision. Despite their idealism, or perhaps on account of it, cooperatives are no less vulnerable to this kind of erosion. Because this is so, I've often suggested that we have a vice president in charge of revolution. He'd be one man not responsible for any operations. He'd stand to one side, with whatever staff he needed, to pick holes in whatever we were doing and remind us of our basic philosophy, our fundamental concepts. His job would be to stir up everything and everybody, to criticize and challenge everything being done—objectives, methods, programs, results. He'd keep us so discontented with the status quo there'd never be any doubt of our desire to seek new ways to meet people's needs. He'd keep us on the right track.

---

7. Quoted in David McCord Wright, "The Administrative Fallacy," *Harvard Business Review*, July-August, 1960, p. 114.

People change whether institutions change or not, and institutions that forget this are left behind. Executives get into ruts. . . . I would want my vice president in charge of revolution to spend time throwing us off balance, shaking us out of our coziness, making us feel a little insecure and uncertain.[8]

Looking ahead, I would predict that long-range planning will find its way further into managerial favor because of its unique value in stirring up fresh attitudes and agitating a group's thinking. By definition, long-range planning implies thinking in a time period beyond the pressure of current events. Freed from the immediate demands of operations and intra-office politics, planners can more seriously question various policies that might never otherwise be disputed. For instance, sometimes a policy of promotion only from within or of remaining first in research in the industry can loom so large in the perspective of day-to-day operations that there seems to be no possibility at all of disputing it seriously except in a completely different context.

A more subtle advantage of planning comes from the process of organizing and rearranging information. For example, the planning group looks at a hodgepodge of facts about customers, decides to classify them by profitability, and learns to its surprise that 85 per cent of the firm's profits come from less than 15 per cent of the customers. Or a man assigned to estimate the volume of future new products pores over a maze of past records and estimates, shuffles and reshuffles the data, and suddenly discovers that there has been a fairly consistent relationship over the years between a dollar invested in research one year and a dollar returned in new product sales five years later. In short, the revelation comes not from the facts themselves but from the effort to classify and relate them in meaningful ways, and this effort is a typical step in long-range planning.

Insistence on putting the productivity of the organization ahead of friendships, sentiment, and traditional ties. President

8.   Murray D. Lincoln, *Vice President in Charge of Revolution* (New York: McGraw-Hill Book Company, Inc., 1960), pp. 296-297.

Lowell of Harvard used to say that one of the most unpleasant tasks of the administrator was that he sometimes had to inflict pain on people. No manager needs to be told what Lowell meant. Often the needs of the organization as a whole do conflict harshly with the interests of individuals, and when that happens and the manager decides in favor of the organization, the unpleasantness he creates is raw and personal and face-to-face. Yet that is the course taken again and again in professional management circles.

It may seem to the observer that, in his cold-blooded pre-occupation with organizational goals, the administrator has no time for friendship. He may dispute the promotions of best friends, deny pay raises desperately needed for family reasons, fire in-laws. His actions *are* cold-blooded in a way—but he does not think of them that way. He thinks of the welfare of the greatest *number* of people, which means the welfare of the organization. In this sense, therefore, his actions are humane and generous, but it is a relatively abstract sense not easily understood by outsiders.

Nevertheless, breaking with sentiment may cause the manager much personal agony. I have known of executives who have been miserable for months following a refusal to a friend in the firm—yet they would have found it almost inconceivable to do anything else. Few men can follow such ruthless dictates of the managerial mind more than part of the time. They will sometimes find ways to rationalize nepotism or assignments to men whom they find congenial. We can only say that in the managerial mind there is a constant *effort* to put creative relationships ahead of other considerations. We cannot claim that the effort always succeeds.

Attention to the search for objective methods and measurements. This attention is a particularly important expression of the aggressive interest in problems. In organizational life, at least, objectivity has connotations of ruthlessness; it means that friendship, kindness and sympathetic "looking the other way" can no longer be counted on to help keep problems hidden. As long as organizations were managed primarily on the basis of personal

alliances, agreements, and power, there was always the possibility
of glossing over problems by mutual consent (as, for example, our
Congressmen for years avoided direct confrontation of the problem of agricultural subsidies and surpluses because of "politics").
With the advent of objectivity this way of operation is threatened.

The tendency of the professional manager is to say, in effect,
"We'll decide it in such-and-such a way, and let the chips fall
where they may." Hence, we find an agency's decision on a
public relations problem depending not on an executive's notion about the situation but on a professional opinion survey.
A marketing program may be held up, not for discussion on a
sales executive's personal argument about what should be done,
but for the results of a rigorously designed market-research study.
Return-on-investment formulas are assuming a stronger and
stronger role in the choice of plant and equipment projects.
Companies are making serious efforts to put price tags on research, industrial relations, personnel, and other types of policy.

The objective approach helps to show where deadly routines
are setting in. It can be used to prick illusions of security and to
show the fallacy of premature conclusions. It has great utility,
furthermore, in helping to develop flexibility of thought. As
Melvin Anshen has noted about mathematical techniques in
particular,

> The intellectual issue to be grasped firmly is the necessity for
> distinguishing between quantitative specificity, on the one hand, and
> accuracy in the sense of identity with true values, on the other.
> Many of us are victims of an educational indoctrination that blurs
> this distinction. The language of mathematics differs from the lan-
> guage of words not because it is inherently and inevitably more ac-
> curate, but simply because it is more manipulatable. Mathematics
> facilitates comparisons not invited by verbal statements.[9]

The return-on-investment analysis may thus help to develop
flexibility of thought by differentiating parts of the problem, by
forcing company people to recognize their various opinions and

9. Melvin Anshen, "Price Tags for Business Policies," *Harvard Business
Review*, January-February, 1960, p. 77.

judgments—in short, by lengthening the lines of discussion and increasing the number of possible "contact points" for argument. Much the same result can be accomplished in other areas by market research, public opinion, research policy, capital budgeting, and other types of analyses that use quantitative measures.

Whenever such situations occur, those involved have a new chance to discard old assumptions and stale ideas. Conflict and tension there may be, without doubt, and certainly some mistaken decisions may result—but it is out of such conditions that the *possibilities* for improvement develop.

It should be emphasized, of course, that the manager or supervisor does not go so far with objectivity as the scientist or engineer does—primarily because the preoccupation of the latter is with problem-solving or truth-seeking. The manager, on the other hand, not only solves problems and makes judgments about the realities of a situation but also concerns himself with questions of desirable goals—of what *should* be. These value judgments cannot be made by quantitative means. In the selection of planning goals, for example, or of the desirable level of service to give customers, the manager will make strong and purposeful use of subjective, intuitive, purely personal judgments. He may use objective methods and tests, but he is likely to fence them off from some crucial areas of the problem.

COPING WITH THE DILEMMAS

Earlier in this book we looked at some of the dilemmas of management. Interest in problems helps in several ways to cope with these dilemmas.

For one thing, a willingness to raise problems in all their dimensions, analyze them objectively, and achieve solutions means the transference of more power to professional and technical people down the line. Let me illustrate with an example of market research. As long as the top executive refuses to recognize that the company has a real problem in identifying new tastes and preferences that *appear* to be affecting sales of present prod-ucts, he monopolizes the decision-making power and uses research assistants as mere pawns in his game. He then falls prey to the corrosive forces described in Chapter 2. If, on the other hand, he does recognize that there is a problem requiring expert diagnosis, then he tends naturally to hand over considerable responsibility to his staff assistants. Indeed, because it is a problem for technical skills, he is likely even to delegate what is actually policy-making authority—the authority to decide what areas of research merit priority, how much validation of results is required, what if any use to make of outside consultants, and so forth. His formal "okay" may be required for these decisions, but his acceptance of the unique capacity of his research assistants leads him to accept most of their technical recommendations. In this case, the vicious cycle described in Chapter 2 is not set in motion.

A second advantage of the problem-seeking attitude is that the more questions an executive raises about operations and proce-dures, the more chances others have to offer ideas of their own and join in the creation of policies. To the extent that they have such chances, they are not merely "used" as means to the boss's ends, since the ends are more likely to be their own, as well as the boss's. Then, too, the more an administrator is alert to problems, the more likely he is to see the results of his own mis-takes, which are less likely to go uncorrected.

But efforts to find problems and turn up weaknesses are per-haps most significant for another reason. An organization in which the need for questioning, argument, and change is ac-cepted is one in which there must necessarily be some give and take between manager and managed. No matter how hard boiled and arbitrary a supervisor is, when he holds problems up to the light, he almost always listens at least for a moment to what somebody else says. He may reject the opinion, but he *hears* it. Hopefully, he will be intrigued enough to raise questions and mull it over.

Accordingly, the problem-seeking attitude reduces the "inhumanity of management." It increases the likelihood that superior and subordinate will have to contend with each other. It keeps the organization from being quite so smooth-running and automatic as it might otherwise be. The "cogs" in the machine say things and are heard; they may even talk back persuasively enough to change what the "operator" is doing.

IMPLICATIONS FOR INDIVIDUALS

What does all this mean for the manager seeking a professional rationale for his approach to his work or for the scientist, accountant, or personnel expert trying to justify transferring into full-time administration? What is the evidence that the administrative approach is more than hard work, "guts," luck, and political "savvy"?

1. *The would-be manager will recognize that the problem-solving orientation is typically professional.* Law, medicine, accounting, and other professions all owe their existence to clients with problems, and their role in the economy is justified by their ability to devise solutions. The manager's "clients" are all those who have a stake in his organization—workers, suppliers, customers, stockholders (in the case of business), the community.

2. *Veteran managers should help others to see that alertness of mind, discernment, analytical ability, and other intellectual traits are absolutely essential.* No amount of honesty, sincerity, loyalty, warmth, or other such attributes can substitute for these traits. Qualities of character, despite their tremendous importance in group behavior, are only part of the picture.

3. *The new manager will find that objectivity—on occasion, cold, aloof, and detached—is no less valuable in administration than in a host of professions and sciences.* In neither case can the practitioner allow himself to become so emotionally involved in a

problem or issue that he loses his perspective and the ability to apply knowledge and experience.

4. *New men will also find that the type of problem-solving ability required is of a more general than special type.* The emphasis is on broad scope rather than on great depth in any one area (note the contrast with staff specialities). The administrator more closely resembles the general practitioner in medicine than the specialist. He is more like the family doctor than the dermatologist.

6

THE

MANAGERIAL

ATTITUDE

TOWARD

MANIPULATION

AN ADMINISTRATOR'S ATTITUDE toward the manipulation of subordinates has momentous consequences for his career, the organization, and society. First, it affects whether or not the work of assistants bears the stamp of his personality or theirs. Sometimes, for instance, when people are discussing a man's actions in the organization, someone will say, "He must have been doing it for old J.B." Old J.B., as everyone knows, does certain things in certain recognizable ways, and he trains everyone else to use his ways too.

Second, his attitude toward manipulation is important because it determines how many people the manager can utilize effectively. Can he successfully direct a large organization or only a small one? How wide a range can he supervise efficiently? The answers depend, at least in part, on his beliefs about controlling people's minds and actions.

Third, the extent to which members of an organization are manipulated affects its general atmosphere and morale. Frustration, guilt, resentment of authority, and self-confidence are all partial outgrowths of the control relations between manager and managed.

Fourth, the extent and quality of manipulation have a bearing on the organization's contribution to the outside world. In the broad sense, each organization is a training ground for the community. Its administrators and workers acquire values and skills that affect their performance when they go on to jobs in other organizations in government, education, or industry. In the long run, of course, the success of any organization is affected by its "organizational environment." Its workers' attitudes toward management are influenced by the attitudes of workers in other firms and agencies. Its managers' attitudes toward work and effort are influenced by managerial values that prevail across the country. Recognition of this fact doubtless lay behind certain policies of Ellis A. Stokdyk, the well known government administrator and leader in the co-operative movement. While he was president of the Berkeley Bank for Cooperatives, he "was continually encouraging staff members to train themselves for larger responsibilities, and he never put his personal interests ahead of theirs. . . . He did not hesitate to encourage key members of his staff to accept outside positions regardless of his need for them in the Bank. He fully appreciated that the influence of the Bank would grow if its employees made good in posts of responsibility with cooperatives." [1]

---

1. Joseph G. Knapp, *E. A. Stokdyk—Architect of Cooperation* (Washington, D.C.: American Institute of Cooperation, 1953), p. 64.

The collective importance of these four factors is intensified by the vast new *potentials* for manipulation that the manager has acquired. There was a day when his communications with subordinates were largely restricted to simple dispatches, personal conversation, and messages passed along by trustworthy assistants. Today, however, hundreds of copies of a memo can be printed and distributed with ease in a matter of a few hours. In addition, there are telephones, training movies, manuals, and a host of other communication devices. What is more, the administrator can tell with unprecedented accuracy how well a message has taken hold in the minds of employees by the many available "feedback" devices—suggestion systems, written reports, personnel office surveys, audits by consultants, and so forth. Then, too, the manager of today is more likely to use at least a smattering of psychology in sizing up the person he wants to influence and applying the appropriate techniques—flattery, fear, appeals to status consciousness, or others. I recently heard of an executive who was studying Communist brainwashing techniques with a view to applying some of them in industrial relations! Modern control techniques—especially those that help management to focus quickly on deviations and aberrations from the norm in a group's performance—should also be mentioned.

It should be clear from this discussion that attitudes toward manipulation are a vital aspect of our inquiry into the nature of the managerial mind. We shall deal in this chapter more with the pragmatic, practical aspects of the topic than with the moral ones, but in action the two cannot be kept separate.

The Spectrum of Control Possibilities

Suppose we were to arrange the possibilities for directing employees in a spectrum. We might divide this spectrum into four main parts, recognizing that each blends imperceptibly into another but that the lines of demarcation do serve to distinguish areas of emphasis. How might the four parts compare in terms of managerial standards?

Force. Rather than try to cajole or manipulate, the manager can resort to force. He can choose the straightforward method of telling people exactly what he wants done and how. He can make no bones about his intention to fire them or refuse raises or to transfer them to unpleasant jobs if they don't comply with his directions. In one case study of a manufacturing firm, a foreman named Tony calls his operators together and lectures them sternly:

The quality here has been terrible. I got a report from the test department that shows wrong connections, wrong components and unsolders. Now that's going to stop. We're going to get the rejects down! I'm putting Helen over here and she's Tony to you! What she says goes! And if anyone doesn't cooperate with her, she'll report to me, and believe me, you'll go right out the door and no questions asked. We're going to improve quality and we're going to do it right away.[2]

This approach has the virtues of clarity, but it also has obvious limitations from the administrative point of view. It drastically curtails what the manager can hope to accomplish. To be on top of a situation every minute, to be able to maintain control down to the last detail, he must shut himself off from many problems, experiences, and people. He must ignore all but that narrow, carefully defined slice of the world that he has chosen to dominate. In the end, therefore, he finds himself practically as limited and constricted as the people he controls. He is likely to find himself blocking rather than contributing to the growth, change, and flexibility that keep the organization alive and vigorous.

Hidden persuasion. A second possibility is tricking people into performance. The manager doesn't let them know (or tries not to let them know) that he is guiding them in a certain way.

---

2. A. Zaleznik, *Foreman Training in a Growing Enterprise* (Boston: Harvard Business School, Division of Research, 1951), p. 154.

He [Tony] believed that *people have to be tricked* to get them to do their work, and he further believed that "psychology" was a particularly effective magic. Psychology was the magic use of words. To illustrate, when Tony wanted to time the operators, who he believed were not keeping up, he felt he had to fool them so that they would not know what he was doing. He therefore set up a chart on a clip board and had each operator call out her position number when she had completed a unit. Tony then placed a tally in the appropriate column in his chart. In the meantime, he held a stop watch hidden beneath the chart and he timed the operators. Tony said to the observer, "I'm doing this for show. What I'm really trying to do is time the girls and I don't want to make them nervous so I'm keeping this chart." Another indication of Tony's belief in the "magic" of "psychology" was the way he asked the girls if they had any problems to bring up after his talk on the need for improving quality. "Now do you have any problems to bring up? Are you having any problems on quality or anything else?" There was no reply and Tony said, "You don't have to worry. I want you to tell me if you have any problems." Again there was no response and Tony asked, "Doesn't anybody have anything to say?" The girls began to smile at this point, but Tony was very serious. He believed that a rule of his magic psychology was to get people to say something after they had been "talked to." It was almost a ritual for Tony and the need for spontaneity held no significance for him.[3]

While this approach assumes that the manager must play upon people's hopes, fears, and values in order to elicit certain behavior from them, it does not involve "brainwashing." The supervisor doesn't play psychiatrist, and he doesn't try to sell them his own beliefs. He simply outfoxes them if he can. Students often bring this orientation to university courses in human relations, administrative practices, and psychology and to their reading. They are not so much concerned with understanding or becoming more adaptable as with learning to manipulate. Consciously or unconsciously, they are applying the habits of men who handle materials to the problem of "handling" people, with the implication that people are to be used as if they were metal or wood.

---

3. *Ibid.*, p. 183.

The trouble with this approach, from the supervisor's point of view, is that people usually don't behave as he expects. Instead of outfoxing them, he himself is outfoxed. Human behavior is so full of complexities and unknown quantities that the manager must be lucky to hit the right combination. Zaleznik shows what can happen when he is not lucky. Commenting on Tony's "psychology," he notes:

> Another problem was added to Tony's load, for the "magic" of psychology failed to accomplish the results desired. He had put his faith in this psychology but he was unable to secure any help from it.[4]

Open persuasion. A more effective approach is more old-fashioned: undisguised persuasion. The manager persuades the salesman to adopt certain attitudes toward the company and his job. He convinces the production supervisor that it isn't "right" to let his operators play cards during a break on the line. He talks the controller into pushing his accountants harder. The virtue of open persuasion is that it leaves matters open to negotiation. Each man has a chance to talk back. The manager has the opportunity to discover that he is wrong or that there is a better solution. Persuasion comes naturally to many managers and is perhaps the most instinctively appealing approach of all.

Still, as we all know, persuasion as it is usually practiced is really a kind of club. While more subtle than force, it is actually pressure with a sharp point. When the manager talks to his production supervisor both are perfectly aware that if the latter does not stop those operators from playing cards he may lose a promotion next year. The salesman knows, despite his boss's politeness and casual manner, that if he doesn't behave as he is told, someone will be found who will. The controller knows that he had *better* push his accountants harder—or else.

Open persuasion thus has many of the disadvantages of the hidden type. People may resent it and balk as the operators balked in Zaleznik's case, although not necessarily so severely.

---

4. *Ibid.*

What is more, the manager who has to persuade people—openly or by indirection—to act in ways he wants them to act labors under the same burden as the user of force. He cannot be everywhere at once, and so he must limit himself to those operations he has time to dominate.

Job assignment. Force, hidden persuasion, open persuasion— each may be necessary from time to time. Every supervisor, I suspect, has repeatedly had to use one or more of them, whether he wanted to or not. But the man with a managerial mind experiences a gnawing discomfort from using any technique of manipulation. He yearns for something better. Is there not another way?

This question brings us to a fourth approach: defining the job and its purpose, picking men carefully and giving them all possible support, then trusting to their own ambition and judgment to see the work through. The boss says, in effect, "Here's a *job* that needs to be done." It may be tough, demanding, or even unpleasant, but that makes no difference. The boss believes that once the other man understands the nature of his mission, he will supply his own motivation and, if technically qualified, do best as "his own boss." It is vital, however, to ensure that the subordinate is never excused from the responsibility for producing according to exacting requirements. In fact, his independence from detailed supervision may even lead to higher expectations.

Managing by task assignment does not, it seems to me, have as much appeal to the manager as does open persuasion. I suspect that the majority of administrators, good ones as well as others, would really *like* to be able to control ways and means. If I am right, the desire springs partly from instinct (few executives and supervisors would, after all, be where they are if they did not have above-average drive and ambition) and partly from concern for efficiency ("As long as we're going to do it, let's do it the best way we know how, not the way some guy happens to want to use"). Nevertheless, a large accumulation of experience in the managerial community—some of it written, but most of it

gathered by observation or word of mouth—warns against manip-
ulative approaches. More and more, the trend has veered toward
a more liberal philosophy of direction and control. Adherents of
this "school," for all their frustrations and setbacks, seem to me
more nearly to represent the attitudes and aspirations of the managerial mind than does any other group.

MANAGING BY JOB ASSIGNMENT

What are the most important assumptions made by the administrator who manages by assigning tasks?

The people who staff the organization are of unequal ability.
The manager makes no naive assumption that everyone is competent, able, and willing. If he did, he could not justify his own
power over the others—and anyway the idea simply does not
correspond to the facts. The manager recognizes that, while each
person may excel in one or more ways, only a few have the
capacity to take over a job and "run with it." He seeks to be as
realistic and discerning about his employees' capacities as he can.
Hopefully, his task assignments will reflect this realism. Within
the limits of the actual assignment, however, he believes in giving
the subordinate discretion and he respects his motives. The exact
range of discretion granted may vary widely, depending on the
type of organization (are the men scientists or truck loaders?),
the manager's familiarity with the situation (does he have a
pretty good idea from past experience of what the problems
are?), the incentives offered, and other factors. But the principle
of granting discretion is the same in all cases.

The manager believes he can pick good men for the job. If he
lacks such confidence, he cannot justify granting considerable discretion to others. This reasoning doubtless has much to do with
the burgeoning literature on psychological tests, performance appraisal, and related topics that appears so frequently in the pages
of management journals and books. It is revealing, I think, that

while managers often fear the consequences of psychological tests (especially, the prospect of an organizational stereotype), they still lean strongly toward using them.[5]

The administrator assumes he is as dependent on other people as they are on him. This assumption is part of the justification for sharing control and authority. If the administrator believed instead that others leaned heavily on him but that he was completely independent of them, he would have an unrealistic view of his power over the organization. He would believe, for one thing, that with a shake of his finger he could make subordinates act in his image. There would not be much point in sharing authority with people who were so dependent on him. The logic of the situation would call instead for his acceptance of absolute responsibility. Fortunately, the professional manager does not view the situation in this way.

"I not only believe in the group," one prominent business leader says of his organization, "I am dependent on it." The administrator assumes that he cannot control the way employees think, nor would he if he could. The general foreman of a department with a fine performance record has remarked:

> Since they [the operators] all know that it's up to them to control their expenses, they do it. If someone from another department comes and tries to borrow something which they know has been charged against their budget, they simply won't allow it. They'll say, "No, you'll run our expense budget over. You'll have to get it somewhere else." I go over the budget with Bill once a month, whenever it comes out. We talk about it. From then on it's up to him. I keep an eye on it every now and then just to see that he isn't running too far out on a limb, and if I see something wrong, I'll ask him about it. But if he feels, he can tell me that he's making out all right, I let him go.[6]

Significantly, this foreman's attitude is shared by many top men in the largest and most powerful organizations. Indeed, the

---

5. Lewis B. Ward, "Putting Executives to the Test," *Harvard Business Review*, July-August, 1960, p. 6.

6. American Radiatronics Corporation (A), a Harvard Business School case. Copyright 1960 by the President and Fellows of Harvard College.

explanation for their success may lie partly in this attitude. By acknowledging their dependence on others, can they not maintain creative relationships with more men and groups than would otherwise be possible?

He believes himself justified in letting the power of creative relationships work in ways that he may not understand. He will not be disappointed if other men's tastes, feelings, and methods differ from his. He expects that they will differ. He knows that it is when people are operating at full capacity, when they are giving the best that is in them, that all the countless variations and complexities and "quirks" of human nature are likely to be most visible.

He therefore may as well save himself the bother of trying to measure interaction precisely. Exactly what effect he is having on others, what effects they are having on one another—these factors are often beyond his comprehension. All he can be sure of is that *in a general way* he can make his influence felt through the power of example, of friendship, of argument and criticism, of mutual goals, of sharing knowledge and experience with others. "He rubs off on you," a man told me once about his boss. "He hardly ever interferes but he's had more effect on me than anyone else in the division. *I don't think he realizes it.*" [Italics added.]

He feels no compunction in placing heavy burdens of judgment and decision-making authority on subordinates' shoulders. The manager can be strict, hard, and "tough-minded" in this respect. He is willing to force his lieutenants, if necessary, to experience the loneliness of command. In an article on General Omar Bradley, A. J. Liebling quoted him as saying:

"You don't even tell a corps or division commander how to do his job when you have an army. You assign a mission, and it's up to the fellow to carry it out. Of course, if you are in a position to have a look and talk it over with the guy, you may make suggestions, but he doesn't have to take them." Bradley was so faithful to this principle that, according to a colonel on General Patton's staff, when he was reduced to a "one-army Army Group" during the Ardennes battle, he declined to interfere with the tactics of that Army, the Third. "It's your army, George," Bradley told Patton, according to the colonel. "You fight it." [7]

Writing about such a relationship from the other side and from a different background, the president of E. I. du Pont de Nemours & Company described his own experience:

When I was elected president, there were still very much on the scene not less than four previous presidents of our Company. All had offices on the same floor as mine, and usually all four were on hand daily.

You might think that, in such a situation, I would not lack for advice or suggestions. Far from it! In my early days of uncertainty, I used to go from one to the other and ask how they would approach this problem or that. I had a terrible time getting any answers at all!

"Well, now, whatever you think," they would say. I would press on, hoping for some concrete thought, some ray of illumination. But only with the greatest reluctance would any of them offer an opinion. Not once has one of them ever come to me with a gratuitous suggestion.

To the man who follows me, I can only say, "From the day you take over, it's up to you. If you want general hints, there is much tradition and some literature. I expect to take my ease and watch you do the work." [8]

Yet, as Greenewalt himself emphasizes in discussing the company organization, the responsibility for what is done resides completely in the senior executives. They cannot "wash their hands" of a man once a mission is assigned. If the job-assignment approach is sometimes tough on a subordinate, it can be very trying for the boss.

The supervisor assumes that it is good for employees to be genuinely concerned about the operations of the enterprise,

---

7. "Five-Star Schoolmaster," *The New Yorker*, March 10, 1951, p. 48. Quoted in John D. Glover and Ralph M. Hower, *The Administrator* (Homewood, Illinois: Richard D. Irwin, Inc., 1957), p. 14.

8. Crawford H. Greenewalt, *The Uncommon Plan* (New York: McGraw-Hill Book Co., Inc., 1959), pp. 12-13.

despite the probability that he himself will have to accept interruptions of his office schedules, "talking back," and conflicts of opinion between managers and workers.

Chris Argyris has shown how an authoritarian management can make workers close their minds to the company interest and perform automatically on their jobs—hard-working but totally disinterested. His study covered "Plant 5," a manufacturing plant with about 500 people. Top management followed a philosophy of close, rigid supervision and control over the activities of foremen and operators. It wanted and expected workers to be dependent on it, subordinate, hard-working, obedient, and so forth. In exchange, management paid well.

The men reacted by applying themselves in a businesslike way but with little concern about the real problems of the plant or the possibilities for showing imagination or taking initiative for improvement. They did not identify themselves with the firm, worry about it, or show interest in its problems. Many said they contributed little more than the abilities needed to run the machines. As one put it with a laugh, "There's not much to me, you might say I'm dead." Skilled and nonskilled workers alike were so unaccustomed to "deep, rich, interpersonal relationships" that only superficial contacts were important to them. In a poll, 65% of the employees, 67% of the foremen, and 90% of the executives reported that they had not formed deep or close personal friendships in the plant, although more than 90% of them had been working there from five to fifty-one years. The researchers were especially impressed by the high number of operators who emphasized that they wanted to be (and were) *left alone* by management. They did not want to be involved.[9]

Such attitudes are anathema to the managerial mind, not because they keep routine work from getting done (they do not interfere with that) but because management is isolated in a sea of dull, apathetic faces. As an organism the firm is half dead.

---

9. Chris Argyris, "The Organization: What Makes It Healthy?" *Harvard Business Review,* November-December, 1958, p. 107.

With the exception of some harried managers, nobody worries about it as long as the pay checks are forthcoming.

For the opposite of the "Plant 5" situation to exist, management of course must pay a price. Its ideas will not always be accepted without argument. For every useful suggestion it receives, several poor ones will probably have to be considered. It will have to put up with actions and reactions that seem ill-advised or make little sense. This incident from a case at the Lincoln Electric Company of Cleveland, Ohio, is an excellent example:

At one time an epidemic of gambling during the lunch hour developed at the plant, and increasingly large sums of money were seen changing hands. The management was much concerned over this because, while the management recognized the freedom of the workers to spend their money and to use their lunch hours as they saw fit, nevertheless it was felt that the morale of the plant was in danger. The management was loath to order the cessation of gambling and to place the burden of enforcement upon the foremen. The management was most anxious not to prejudice the good relations existing between the foremen and the workers by placing the foremen in the position of enforcing what might be a highly personal and perhaps unpopular ruling.

Nor was the company willing to place the burden of enforcement on the plant guards and watchmen for fear of impairing the relations between this group and the workers.[10]

As it happened, the president of the company presented his point of view on the problem to the advisory board, made up of representatives from all over the plant. The board took the matter under advisement but never made a recommendation because the workers heard of it and solved the problem quickly by putting pressure on the gambling ringleaders to stop. Note that the president knew from past experience that neither the advisory board nor the workers felt any obligation to agree with him. He trusted that the process of sharing concern would work in its own way,

---

10. Observations on the Lincoln Electric Company, Harvard Business School case. Copyright 1947 by the President and Fellows of Harvard College.

which might or might not have been the way for which he hoped.
Certainly he had some anxious moments.

*The manager assumes that most people like to be challenged
to use their ingenuity and that, in taking this approach, he does
not risk his effectiveness or popularity.* He assumes that asking
a normally healthy person to use his head will not panic or
upset him but that the assignment will be welcomed. The assignment may create problems, and it may lead to some worry and
griping, but it will be respected.

It is this assumption that often leads managers to depart from
the ways of "scientific management" and from what the psychol-
ogist calls highly "structured" work assignments (in which every
process is already carefully defined for the worker). A food-store
executive has supplied an illustration from his experience:

> There are three steps in wrapping a package of self-service meat:
> weighing, printing the label, and wrapping. Among different girls
> there will be different aptitudes; one task calls for visual acuity,
> another for finger dexterity, and so on. Under "scientific manage-
> ment" bosses would assign the functions to separate individuals. Yet
> I have observed that when the five or six girls in a wrapping room
> are permitted to vary and rotate the tasks among themselves by
> their own plan or lack of plan, morale and production will im-
> prove.[11]

The higher the level of authority, the more freedom is likely
to be given. Indeed, to men of Frederick Taylor's school it might
appear that executives in many organizations today are delegating
with abandon—and in a sense they are.

*The manager assumes that he can be loyal to the organization
and to the people in it without having to agree with people's decisions about the way they do their jobs.* In other words, simply
because he is dedicated to the life of the organization does not
mean that he cannot tolerate activities that he personally considers ill-advised or wrong. Everybody does not have to be doing

---

11. Paul Cifrino, "The Mainspring of Business Leadership," *Harvard
Business Review,* September-October, 1956, p. 59.

things "right" in his view. The answers his subordinates come up with do not have to be the same as his own. The principle was stated this way by one of the staff executives under Eugene M. Zuckert, when he was Assistant Secretary of the Air Force:

> I suppose we are question-raisers mostly. We see things which don't seem to make sense, and then we start asking questions of the staff section which is concerned with it. Sometimes we have to keep asking questions until they really start to take hold. When they're working on the problem they may ask us to help and then we do. *But it is their problem and their answer.* When it has been approved and coordinated by the Staff and comes up to [the Assistant Secretary of the Air Force (Management)] we check on it again and ask some more questions. But most of the time it's pretty well worked out by then. We try to get them to carry the ball all the way so that it's their answer when it's over.[12]

This approach is an essential part of the rationale of accountability. In one top executive's words, "Unless we are willing to grant our managers the freedom of *how* the job is to be done —then we are never in a position to say that they failed. If we ourselves assume the responsibility of defining the *how,* then we can no longer hold them accountable." [13]

The manager or supervisor assumes that he cannot really put himself in another employee's place. He may succeed in understanding another man's position and appreciating his feelings, but he cannot see the world through that person's eyes. The manager who makes this assumption finds it natural to define the area of "other people's business" more generously than he otherwise might. He may be convinced that Jones could do better if he would assert himself more and be less retiring. He may see with great clarity that Jordan ought to brush off his overbearing wife and make his own decisions. He may wish with all his heart

12.   John D. Glover and Paul R. Lawrence, *A Case Study of High Level Administration in a Large Organization* (Boston: Harvard Business School Division of Research, 1960), p. 64. Italics added.

13.   William T. Brady, "The Freedom to Make Mistakes," an address to the Top Management Seminar on Executive Practices and Methods, 1959 (Corn Products Company, New York), p. 9.

that Jenkins would stop smoking and drinking so much since he is obviously suffering ill effects. But how does he know whether friendly words of advice to Jones will help him or make him even more passive and timid? How can he know how it feels to be in Jordan's place? And how can he know what deep and hidden reasons may drive Jenkins to excessive smoking and drinking? The needs that drove him to drink might be intensified by the manager's interference.

In short, the manager feels that if he would have any influence at all, he must recognize his own limitations. The simple tools and measures that are his—hiring, firing, job assignments, productivity analysis, quality standards, and the rest—he will use with vigor and enthusiasm. But if he overreaches or develops illusions of grandeur, he may well end with no control at all.

Permissible Exceptions to the Rule

Executives and supervisors do not consider it possible to avoid manipulation all the time, and they wouldn't if they could. There are times when intrusion is justified. For example, the manager often considers episodes like this one, recounted by the Chairman of the Board of American Brake Shoe Company, permissible and even desirable:

I had an experience which will always be vivid in my memory. The man involved was an outstanding salesman from one of our midwest offices. He had an invalid wife and three young children. He called to say he had given up striving to keep sober in the United States and was off to a job in a distant country. He would send home as big a part of his pay check as possible. He wanted to thank me for the number of times we had taken him back and helped with the bills.

This attractive, able fellow had decided to "beat it" as an escape from the temptations of friends. His wife would stay home with the children, their sicknesses, the shortages of cash which were there and were ahead, and all the other troubles of such a family, and meet alone her unshared responsibilities.

I said to him, "You won't do that. You won't run out on your great responsibilities. Your friends think well of you. You have all kinds of ability. Are you yellow? If not, you must realize it is not possible for you to follow this plan. If not, you will be back here in my office tomorrow morning. The company will re-offer you the job from which you've been fired four times, pay your family debts, and re-establish the pay rate you received before being fired the first time."

I went home that night hopeful and also grateful to him for not having taken a swing at me.[14]

Sometimes intrusions of this kind are justified on the grounds of compassion. The simple, impulsive desire to help bursts through the bounds of habit and policy, often succeeding simply because the desire is so pure and spontaneous. Regardless of the explanation, however, it is reasonable to argue that some questions— what is manipulation and what isn't? what is intrusion and what isn't? what is interference and what isn't?—cannot be answered in the abstract because so much depends on relationships between people and on their personalities. How close are their friendships? How congenial are they? What events bring them together?

"You find that there are circles, circles that go out from an inner one," says Duncan E. Littlefair. "The further out you go, the less creative, the less rich, the less deep and the less meaningful are your relationships. When you treat someone way on the outside as though he were here in the inner core, you're doing violence, not only to yourself, but to this person who is a stranger. When you treat people who are really in this inner circle the same way you treat a person that you don't know, you're doing violence, great violence, to your spirit and to the spirit of the other person. . . . You have degrees of interaction. You have degrees of liability and responsibility. You have degrees and levels of intimacy and understanding." [15]

---

14. William B. Given, Jr., *Reaching Out in Management* (New York: Harper & Brothers, 1953), p. 55. The man did not return to Brake Shoe, but he did return to his family and straighten himself out.

15. Duncan E. Littlefair, *The Principle of Non-Intrusion*, a series of extemporaneous sermons (Grand Rapids, Michigan: Fountain Street Baptist Church, 1952), p. 49.

From time to time, therefore, the man with a managerial mind can be found lecturing someone about his personal habits, advising about attitudes toward the boss, or arguing about the way private offices should be kept—when such behavior is not at all necessary from an organizational point of view. The demand is made, the question is asked, the advice is given out of an intuitive knowledge that at this time, with this person, in this way it is completely proper.

While these exceptions to the attitude about control and interference do not occur very often, they can be extremely important in raising the quality of support that managers and workers give one another—occasionally as important as the main attitude itself.

TOLERANCE FOR WASTE AND INEFFICIENCY

How much waste and inefficiency do these managerial attitudes involve? A good deal—which is amazing since the conventional economic or "scientific management" point of view holds that the manager must use every possible angle to achieve efficiency, especially in business. The explanation, of course, is that when an executive tries to achieve efficiency by insisting that everyone perform in a certain way, without mistakes, he opens the floodgates to an even greater and more devastating type of waste—the waste of people's abilities, drains on initiative, and the others mentioned in Chapter 2.

What kinds of waste, specifically, does the managerial mind acknowledge as often necessary—or even desirable? One kind is simple everyday errors of procedure or mistakes in judgment. An attorney in the tax bureau insists that he can crack a certain case of suspected tax evasion, and, although his boss has doubts, he lets him go ahead anyway because of his enthusiasm and ability. A quarterback wants to open the game with a series of pass plays, and the coach doesn't think it's going to work but lets him go ahead because of the way the player's eyes are lit up. A salesman is using last year's flip charts despite the territorial supervisor's objections, and the supervisor overlooks it because the man seems able to learn a lot from experience.

The instances are ordinary, but it is not so easy to stand aside as it may sound. From a managerial point of view, it may be agonizingly difficult at times. The head of Johnson & Johnson testified that:

> The most frustrating experience is to stand aside and observe a mistake and to make no move to correct it. But we frequently find that the man making an error discovers it himself, before the mistake comes to full fruition. If he does make this discovery, he has certainly learned a lesson for life. If he is stopped by even the most persuasive executive, he will believe that he was right and, had he been privileged to carry his program to conclusion, all would have been well. At times men do carry mistakes to ultimate failure, but usually these failures are not catastrophic either to the organization or to the men.
>
> What I am describing—what I believe we are practicing to some degree in our companies—is really nothing more than providing opportunities for new experiences through learning by doing, with limited guidance, but freedom of operation to the individual executive.[16]

What makes it more difficult still, of course, is that what the other man learns by doing is not necessarily what the boss *thought* he would learn or what the boss himself once learned. Here is another example, this one from the autobiography of the founder of a great co-operative:

> I know that I have caused the organization a great deal of loss and injury because I won't stop a man the first instant I learn he is doing something wrong. I would rather allow him to discover for himself that he has gone wrong. I know it is a costly method, but I believe it is the only acceptable one for at least two reasons. The first reason is that I'm sure it takes a fairly arrogant man to assume that he knows better than anyone else how a job should be

---

16. Robert W. Johnson, "Executive Freedom," Edward C. Bursk, ed., *How to Increase Executive Effectiveness* (Cambridge: Harvard University Press, 1953), p. 21.

done. I do not pretend to know more than the next man. I hesitate to correct him in the performance of a job which is, after all, his responsibility. The second reason is that if the man in question has gone far enough wrong to satisfy me that he is wrong but not far enough to satisfy himself, a correction from me or from his superior is going to destroy a fraction of his independence. In addition, it's going to instill in him a resentment based on the feeling that he was right and would have been able to demonstrate it if he had not been prematurely checked. An expensive process, I admit, but one that does save executives from being ruined, that does save people from becoming embittered and unhappy and ultimately useless. After all, an organization that is designed to meet people's needs ought to take into account the needs of the people who work for it.[17]

THE PERSONAL CHALLENGE

Managing by the job assignment puts more, rather than less, pressure on the executive to win respect for his judgment and knowledge from associates and juniors. If he is running everything with a tight rein, the tendency is for his people to knuckle under, to do what they are told, and stop asking questions. The foremen and workers in Chris Argyris's "Plant 5," for example, didn't do much thinking on the job. In such circumstances, there may be a good deal of complaint and resentment about the boss's directives, but since he is the only one who is genuinely concerned with the whole situation, he should have no trouble in overwhelming anyone in an argument.

If, however, his policies require others to do a good deal of thinking and worrying too, he has more "competition." When he does intrude, as sometimes he must, his judgments come under a harsher spotlight. Others have been thinking on their own. Evaluations are keener. Here is one reason that the managerial mind frequently finds itself under pressure to master details and concepts, to have wide knowledge, to be ready with quick and

---

17. Murray D. Lincoln, quoted in David Karp, *Vice President in Charge of Revolution* (New York: McGraw-Hill Book Company, Inc., 1960), p. 303.

discerning questions. Without having earned solid respect for his acumen, the manager finds it difficult to interfere successfully when he does interfere, and his refusals to control have less meaning. This later point is of especial significance for a liberal philosophy of delegation. The more highly regarded a superior is, the more pressure he can put on a subordinate to do his best when decisions *are* left to him. A case in point is the relationship between Generals Lee and Jackson in the Civil War, Lee being the respected "boss" who gave his lieutenant great latitude in tactical decisions. The following incident occurred during a meeting of the two at the Fredericksburg front in April, 1863:

Jackson was awake early at his camp and from the first hour was full of fight. Together with Lee he observed the Federal dispositions and discussed the proper tactics. The commanding General [i.e. Lee] was quite clear in his own mind: It was better to await the enemy's attack, if one was to be delivered. . . .

Jackson had abundant reason for knowing this, in the light of what had happened to his advancing batteries on the evening of December 13, but he could not bring himself to forgo the chance of striking an enemy who was hugging a river bank [the Rappahannock River]. As Jackson stood unconvinced, Lee spoke again: "If you think it can be done, I will give orders for it."

That put the onus on Jackson. Willing as always he was to make decisions, he was loath to go squarely against the judgment of the man whom, as he had told Boteler, he was "willing to follow blindfolded." Jackson asked now for more time in which to examine the terrain. Lee at once assented. Most of a rainy afternoon Jackson then spent in more detailed study of the ranges, the gun positions, the ground across which his troops must sweep to reach the Federals. At length and most regretfully, he had to own to himself that an advance would be costly and that withdrawal would have to be under a devastating fire.[18]

It is probably safe to say that if "Stonewall" Jackson hadn't been so afraid that Lee was right, he wouldn't have been so anxious to double-check himself. But if in Lee's place at that moment there had been an officer like Beauregard or Toombs,

---

18.   Douglas Southall Freeman, *Lee's Lieutenants: A Study in Command*, Vol. 2 (New York: Charles Scribner's Sons, 1944), pp. 526-527.

whose judgments Jackson did not happen to respect, it is probable that there would have been no poring over the maps on a rainy afternoon. Nonintrusion would not have had the same effect at all.

It must be emphasized that the value of this approach as a technique is not that it convinces others to do what the manager wants them to do. Lee was not using a psychological ruse in the foregoing case—he was simply stating as a matter of plain fact that he would support Jackson's advance if requested. The point is that the approach doesn't work so well—the manager does not *challenge* an associate so much—if he has not himself set high standards for the associate.

ECCE HOMO

Few attitudes of the managerial mind are so likely to cause trouble for the administrator as the desire to strike a balance between control and no control, between intrusion and delegation. The balance is never perfect, and there is no formula for making it perfect. Even in the most ideal circumstances, the manager is bound to err, going too far at one time, not far enough at another. He second-guesses himself and is subject to much second-guessing from others. He may be right for the wrong reasons and wrong for unforeseeable reasons, so that the lessons from experience are never quite clear.

Furthermore, many of his actions involve a terrible finality. So often there is no drawing back, no possibility of revision once control has been handed over. What mental anguish may result, both before and after the act of delegation! Harking back to some of the examples in this chapter, one can imagine Lee's emotions had Jackson gone ahead with the advance on the Federals and lost half his division. One can picture the misery of senior executives at Du Pont when a younger, newer man whom they have refused to direct comes up with a real "turkey." One can visualize the anxieties that top management at Lincoln Electric would have continued to suffer if, after they had decided not to interfere in the gambling situation, the workers had been happy to let it go on.

In such circumstances the best-intentioned of men can make fools of themselves by deviating from their original decisions. In Shakespeare's *King Lear,* the old ruler hands his kingdom over to two daughters but, out of habit, goes on behaving as if he were still king. The eldest daughter, Goneril, can scarcely endure this behavior, and, on one of his visits to her castle, she blurts out:

> Idle old man
> That still would manage those authorities
> That he hath given away! Now, by my life,
> Old fools are babes again . . .

Yet the man with the managerial mind goes on, cowed a little by his failures but fortified by his successes. And his successes are likely to be impressive, measured in organizational terms. While the attitude toward manipulation and intrusion is one of the most uncertain described in this book, it nevertheless lies behind the administrator's supreme contribution to the organization: strengthening its ability to survive when he departs. The organization may be buffeted and damaged by adversity, but with a hard core of dedicated, enterprising employees it will be able to repair the damage and go on. While its management, like all managements, will be self-defeating to an extent, distrust of manipulation will help to make the *net* gain as great as possible.

In no other respect is the difference between managers and "leaders" more clear. Great leaders do not always leave strong organizations. Great managers do.

IMPLICATIONS FOR INDIVIDUALS

Now let us turn briefly again to the manager or prospective manager concerned with the quality, calibre, and scope of administrative thinking. What implications can he draw from the attitude toward manipulation?

1. *If the management does not want to manipulate employees, then it is more important than ever to understand them.* Actions must be based on sound knowledge and insights about behavior, or the department or work group will "run away" from the aspiring manager. He will be forced to abdicate or bring it under close surveillance (thus lowering his effectiveness as an administrator, as we have seen). The distrust of manipulation is an important factor indeed in the rise of the learned approach to administration and of "egghead" managers.

2. *It is helpful to have the kind of disposition that enables one to gamble on people.* Being able to bring oneself to take a chance on a subordinate—e.g., by throwing him a tough job and letting him run with it—is as important a form of risk-taking in administration as betting on a new product or on a new production process. As William B. Given, Jr., former head of American Brake Shoe Company, used to say, "Some like to gamble at the races or at cards. I like to gamble on people."

3. *The student should be forewarned that most so-called "scientific" approaches to administration miss the point.* The *study* of management is, of course, essential, but the kind of rationalization comparable to that of the applied sciences fails because it is based on "materials thinking" rather than on "people thinking." Cause and effect are closely meshed in the former but not in the latter. In this respect, the administrative point of view more nearly resembles certain humanistic and religious ones, emphasizing the uniqueness and mystery of the individual.

4. *Contrary to many impressions created by loose talk, the new administrator cannot simply carry over into supervision the human-relations practices he may have learned at home.* In countless homes and social groups, manipulation and intrusion are encouraged. A value is put on "controlling" a child or "managing" a wife. The realities of the managerial situation differ from these ideas as the realities of the law differ from inaccurate hearsay about law repeated by the man on the street.

5. *It is useful to be able to accept a good deal of mystery and indefiniteness in work relationships.* Since creative relationships operate in ways the manager often doesn't understand, he will obviously be happier if he can live with surprises, disappointments, and unfathomable turns and twists of human nature. If results are always those he anticipates, something is wrong!

6. *There is a logical, self-reinforcing pattern in managerial thinking despite the many inconsistencies and contradictions of the world managers work in.* In this chapter, we have turned more to the manager's individual, personal relations with subordinates than in previous chapters, where there was more emphasis on dealing with groups. The attitude toward manipulation contains many of the "seeds" of attitudes previously described, yet has a form and significance all its own that bolster the other attitudes.

7

THE

MANAGER'S

EXPECTATIONS

In most fields and vocations other than management, men rely greatly on well-defined expectations. For example, the lawyer thinks in terms of the reciprocal duties of parties to a contract and leans heavily on precedent to predict a court's decision on a case. The scientist values laws of physics and chemistry, that teach him to expect the elements to act and react in certain predictable ways. The accountant follows certain rules for handling assets and income, and he expects business and government to accept his figures so long as he follows those rules. The market researcher picks a sample of respondents carefully and expects that the "universe" of people represented by this sample will act or react in the same way.

In all of these cases, a man's thinking is governed by his expectations. In a sense, his special skill is that he knows exactly what to expect.

Administrators also make great use of expectations. They have expectations of what machines will do, of the effects of economic trends, of cost-volume relationships, of how certain customers or legislators will react, and similar factors. Thanks in part to behavioral research, they also develop expectations of how people and groups will react *on the whole*.

In his relationships with his subordinates, however, the man with a managerial mind does a curious about-face. Instead of welcoming averages, norms, and other expectations, he now becomes impatient with them. He does not deny the record of the past, but he is discontented with it. Often, indeed, he will openly flaunt and violate expectations based on past experience.

This attitude may have extraordinary consequences. It has much to do with the capacity of organizations to excel in old fields and lead the way in new ones. It has much to do with the fact that the study of organizational life amounts to more than an examination of directives, regulations, contracts, "locker-room rules," and so forth, important as they may be for other purposes. Accordingly, we are justified in singling out this attitude —which, let us emphasize, involves only one side of the administrative problem—for study in this chapter.

Burden on the Individual

An expectation, according to the dictionary, involves "grounds on which something is expected to happen." It implies discerning use of the past to outline the future; it implies memory, knowledge, and experience.

While in many ways a person draws support from the past, in some vital respects he is corrupted by it. Why aren't memories and the lessons of experience always valuable?

At the risk of oversimplification, let us take some everyday examples. An office manager finds one day that, if he prefaces a conversation with a clerk by inquiring about the man's family or his golf game, he can put him in a "co-operative mood" or a "receptive state of mind" for a suggestion. He therefore develops the habit of beginning talks by asking, "How's the family?" or "Get in any golf last weekend, Joe?" Pretty soon it is routine with him. He is not asking because he cares but because he wants to be more popular and influential. He "knows what to expect of people." A production man hears that the way to convince the sales department is to get tough and shout and pound the table. He tries it, and it works. He therefore makes a habit of it, not because he is always genuinely excited but because it is "the way to handle those sales boys."

One could go on with such examples, but the point is already clear. In each case, the man is selling both himself and others short because of his oversimplified expectations. How long does the office manager go on fooling everyone with his transparent technique of building "rapport"? How many times does the production man shut out from his mind better ways of convincing the sales department! What is more, when we expect others to act in certain ways, we make it harder for them to find fulfillment. The more power we have over them, the more burdensome our expectations become. "Jake is only good at selling the industrial market," we say. Or "Miss Carter is no good with figures, she couldn't handle that job." Or "Perkins has the ability, but he won't put out on weekends in a pinch so we better not . . . " We put the pressure on the other man to be what we expect him to be. If he wants to make a breakthrough, it is that much harder for him. He gets few chances to demonstrate other capacities, and when he does, the results are viewed with bias. Soon—perhaps much too soon—he himself becomes convinced of his limitations. In short, we prove that what we think we know about people or ourselves is true by forcing it to be true.

Much of the time, to be sure, the other person may be unable to surpass our expectations, or he may not want to even if he can. *Some* of the time, however, he may be both willing and able, and that "some of the time" makes a big difference in an organization because it exerts so much leverage on spirit and morale. Knowing the value of this leverage, the manager is distrustful of placing people in neat patterns. It is revealing, I think, that executives often recount with delight how various men and women they have known put their too-modest judgments to shame. The founder of Nunn-Bush Shoe Company reminisces about one such incident:

Our porter was Jim Clark, a Negro, who like some of his underprivileged race gave no outward indication of possessing either energy or ambition. I was surprised one day when he stopped me in the factory and bluntly, but politely, asked if he could have a raise. I hardly knew what to say at first because I did not want to hurt his feelings; yet I believed he was being paid all he was worth —and all he could ever be worth.

"Jim," I said, "I know that you are not being paid much, and it is not my purpose to criticize, but you are just naturally slow and cannot be different. Frankly, I don't think you are worth any more." I illustrated to him by action how slowly he walked and with what a leisurely motion he swept the floor. My purpose was to justify his small pay, with no thought of changing his ways.

Jim looked at me in amazement. He seemed to have no realization that his actions were as I had indicated, and he accepted my explanation in silence.

The next day as I was walking down the factory steps Jim passed me going up on the run—two steps at a time. Later I noticed him in the cutting room sweeping the floor as if he were engaged in a race, and he kept up his change of attitude, without prompting, as long as I remained in Cape Girardeau. Jim got his raise, and he taught me a lesson.

I wonder how many men and women go through life doing much less than their best because their ability has been underrated and they do not realize their own capabilities.[1]

This incident was a case of low expectations. High expectations can be burdensome, too. Many observers are familiar with instances of people laboring in vain to do things that they can't and don't really want to do because their superiors who "know" they can do them have put them under such severe pressure. As we shall see presently, however, if expectations must be imposed at all, it is better that they be too ambitious than too modest.

---

1. Henry L. Nunn, *The Whole Man Goes to Work* (New York: Harper & Brothers, 1953), pp. 136-137.

VALUED APPROACHES

How does the managerial mind react to these difficulties? What specific attitudes and approaches are favored? In the next few pages, we shall examine some of the most significant attitudes. The fact they are valued by the administrator does not necessarily mean, however, that they are useful from other points of view. As a matter of fact, I suspect it could be effectively argued that these attitudes of the managerial mind contribute an element of strain and uncertainty in organizational life that—to some, at least—seems far from desirable.

The manager favors efforts to push, prod, or coax the individual to break old patterns and enlarge his horizons. The problem is to get the individual to go beyond his familiar range, to take on work he is not sure he can control. The past must be challenged at every step. The need is familiar to many people concerned with creative relationships. In the words of Duncan E. Littlefair,

The only way you see something new is to have a need to see something new, to be forced to see it. That means you have to wrestle with something you don't like. The only way to get new friends is by being uncomfortable for a while, breaking the mold, getting out of the pattern, transcending the limit, blowing up the system, violating your order and your efficiency and your management, exposing yourself to the abyss, to the destructive, to the unknown, to the transcendental, to that which is beyond you, to what you don't like.[2]

Realizing this need, some managers have made skillful use of their prerogatives to assign jobs.

One of the ways to get people to reach out is to give them missions beyond their area—new experiences. When, for example, our labor relations head was going to St. Louis, he was asked to take a look at our foundry flasks. A castings salesman going to Pittsburgh was asked to inquire among his customers about air compressor

---

2. Duncan E. Littlefair, "How Much Can You Manage?" (Grand Rapids, Michigan: Fountain Street Baptist Church, January 24, 1960), p. 8.

needs. In both suggestions, a new eye with a different focus had been needed, as it often is. The individual himself, however, may feel inhibited because of his lack of previous experience. This makes it even more important for management to suggest his possibilities to him.[3]

Note the difference between this kind of action and manipulation as discussed in Chapter 6. Here the manager is not intruding into another person's personality or trying to control him. To be sure, he is saying, "This sort of thing is good for you." But he does not try to control what the person does or what he gains from the new experience. In the last case, for example, Given was not trying to maneuver the labor relations head into another job or to use the castings salesman to show up the air-compressor salesmen. He was not trying to run a puppet show. He *was* trying to make those men lift their eyes and look over the ridge. What they saw, what they thought, what if any change they underwent —all was left to chance.

"A man's reach should exceed his grasp," wrote Robert Browning, and many managers would agree. Too practical and pragmatic of mind to be much interested in unattainable goals, they may nevertheless put great store in goals that men have to *reach* for, that are not within the certain grasp of ordinary effort but are attainable with intelligent, aggressive effort. When Ellis A. Stokdyk was Deputy Governor in charge of research for the Farm Credit Administration in the 1930's, he gave one of the men on his staff, Harry Trelogan, a job that the man felt he was not equipped to handle. The task was beyond his reach, Trelogan argued. Stokdyk exclaimed: "Harry, you forget whether or not you can do this job. I say you can. Let me be the judge." Stokdyk's belief in people, reports Joseph G. Knapp, made them perform miracles.[4]

---

3. William B. Given, Jr., "Reaching Out in Management," *Harvard Business Review,* March-April, 1952, p. 43.

4. Joseph G. Knapp, *Stokdyk: Architect of Cooperation* (Washington, D. C.: American Institute of Cooperation, 1953), p. 91.

To illustrate in a different context, here is a brief excerpt from a well-known case on the Gray Manufacturing Company (manufacturer of office dictation machines) :

Key to the successful growth of the company, according to each of Mr. Ditmars' subordinates, was Mr. Ditmars himself: his skills, his capacity for hard work, and his zealous attention to company activities. His subordinates reported that "you can watch things explode when Mr. Ditmars arrives at his office." They said his way of operating put a high premium on the ability to think ahead and plan for any contingency. One officer recalled that for several years a motto had hung on Mr. Ditmars' wall, to the effect that the successful executive is one who dreams up impossible jobs for his company and then hires bright young men to do those jobs.

Mr. Ditmars said . . . "My job is to think—and to come up with ideas that will make my men work like hell. My job is also to pick key men for key positions. I believe in surrounding myself with young men who are smarter than I am in their respective fields. I think you will agree that I've succeeded." [5]

The tendency of the managerial mind is to refuse to acknowledge the limitations that people believe they have.

The reasons people underrate themselves are, of course, extremely varied. They include inferiority complexes and simple lack of appreciation of changing conditions that make high-level attainment possible. Uninspired goals may also reflect bargaining strategy. Bruce Payne, the management consultant, was conferring with a division manager of a medium-sized corporation about planning problems. "We were discussing the targets which the division was going to report to the New York office, and in a frank moment the manager happened to remark, 'Of course, I set my goals as low as I can get them.' " According to Payne, this intentionally low pegging of goals is a prevalent tendency in industry because subordinates figure that they get credit for *over*shooting targets, not undershooting them. [6] What he might have

5. Gray Manufacturing Company, Harvard Business School case. Copyright by the President and Fellows of Harvard College.

6. Bruce Payne, "How to Set Realistic Profit Goals," *Harvard Business Review,* September-October, 1958, p. 90.

added is that, while understating capacity may be only a bargaining maneuver at first, if it is continued long and convincingly enough, a man may end up selling *himself* on his limitation, too.

This possibility gives the manager even more reason to question the limitations his people profess. Hopefully, he will be right often enough to keep his skepticism alive and, if he is fortunate, to make himself revered by those he encouraged. One day in the 1920's, when George Borg (of Borg-Warner Corporation) was managing a plant that made clutches for midwestern automobile manufacturers, he called his superintendent, a man named Hartley, and the department heads into his office for a conference.

"We're going to have to make this clutch more cheaply," he said. "I don't mean that we're going to make a cheap clutch. But if we're going to stay alive we're going to have to cut production costs in two."

The shop foremen and engineers looked at him blankly.

"They're pretty low right now," observed Hartley.

"They're as low as we can get them with this construction," agreed Borg. "So we're going to have to try something else. That's what I called you in here for. I want you to get together and figure out a scheme for making the entire clutch out of sheet metal stampings. If we can bat these things out on a punch press without harming their efficiency we can lick the field."

Carl W. [George Borg's father and part owner of the company], who had come to Chicago for the opening of the plant, seemed interested but as usual skeptical.

"Punch press!" he repeated acidly. "You honestly think we can cut 'em like cookies when we busted our necks getting out forty a day for Jeffrey?"

"I think you can make anything on a press that you can make in a mold," said George. "We've got engineers here to find out how. I honestly think they can do it. And I honestly think that if we can make a clutch to sell for about three dollars we can stay in business forever."

The old man shook his head.

"Eighteen dollars to three dollars," he muttered. "And you do it with a slide rule. I'm going back to Moline." [7]

---

7. Robert J. Casey, *Mr. Clutch* (New York: The Bobbs-Merrill Company, 1948), pp. 157-158.

A few days later, George Borg called another conference and asked what progress had been made on his scheme to make clutch parts on a punch press. Here is the report:

> Hartley acted as spokesman for the group.
> "We've gone into it pretty thoroughly, Mr. Borg," he said. "And we don't believe it can be done."
> George looked out the window for a time, then swung around suddenly in his chair.
> "Well," he said quietly. "If you're convinced that you can't do it, then I'll have to get some fellows in here who can."
> "There's no use doing that," said Hartley. "If anybody can do it, we can. We'll give it another try."
> "O.K.," said George. "Try it again—and try harder." [8]

As the reader might guess, Hartley and his men succeeded in this case. But what if they had not? I doubt that Borg's philosophy would have changed much; the attitude toward expectations is partly a matter of faith and does not have to be continually confirmed by experience. There might never have been a Borg-Warner, though, if Borg's plant hadn't been so successful.

The manager tries to create an atmosphere that will encourage venturesomeness and, in particular, freedom from precedent. Of course, almost every executive in business, government, and education is dedicated to the *principle* of venturesomeness. What distinguishes the man with a managerial mind is the emphasis he puts on actually putting the principle into practice.

In his everyday conversation and memoranda he is likely, for example, to show a healthy disrespect for precedent and traditional expectations. The fact that absenteeism in the Los Angeles bureau was only 3% last year, which was then considered good, does not necessarily mean it is good this year. The fact that high loan losses in a certain department have always been considered justified in the past does not necessarily mean they can be so justified again. The fact that a man has always shown a superb sense of public relations does not necessarily mean that,

---

8. *Ibid.*, p. 160.

in the future, he shouldn't try to be pretty good at financial matters too. The head of a lumber yard says,

> I have also found it important to avoid giving people a label. For example, a few years ago we bought a small company and inherited a bookkeeper about 30 years old whom we kept on the job while the transition was being made. Afterward there was no place for him; he did not want to move to our accounting department which is in another city. About that time a manager of a small yard quit and we had a job to fill. Somebody made the very dubious suggestion that we put on the job this bookkeeper who had had no previous experience of this kind. The happy ending here is that a very average bookkeeper has turned out to be one of our best yard managers.[9]

Managers with this point of view imply that the less impressed a supervisor is with the expectations of former years—his own, his organization's—the more freedom he can give others to experiment, innovate, and break with precedent, thus surpassing the expectations of those who did take them seriously. Naturally this philosophy is not easy to practice. The supervisor can, for example, make himself the despair of his employees. "We've always done it in such-and-such a way, we were counting on doing it that way again!" they exclaim. "Why does he always have to change things?" But there will also be those who benefit:

> I asked a young manager who had reached the top quickly what single thing helped him most in his rather brilliant career. He thought awhile, then said, "One thing stands out; I could think out loud with my superiors. I could throw out crazy suggestions. I could talk over any subject without fear that I would be squelched. It had more effect upon my development as a manager than anything else." [10]

Closely related is the assumption that for many men the internal incentive to do well is stronger than such external incentives as directives, reprimands, penalties for failure, or censure

---

9.   John H. Martin, "How to Increase Your Own Administrative Effectiveness," in Edward C. Bursk, ed., *How to Increase Executive Effectiveness* (Cambridge: Harvard University Press, 1953), pp. 132-133.

10.   Frederick C. Crawford, "Creating the Proper Climate," p. 13.

for not conforming with the group. The assumption is that such men are so keenly motivated—so sensitive to their expectations of themselves—that only the broadest, most general, most diffuse type of expectation from a boss is necessary to make them go all out. In my reading of the works of entrepreneur-type managers —the "take-charge" men—I have been so impressed by the frequent outcroppings of this attitude that I want to offer two quite diverse illustrations of its wide range.

From letters (1886–1887) of a senior officer of the Bank of Australasia to the Superintendent, who was criticized for regulating too closely:

A man cannot do more than a day's work in a day, continuously, and as I look at the present circular orders and memoranda I feel that if I were a Branch Manager or officer I should have to choose between neglecting some of them and doing no efficient work at all. If I felt that I must attend to all orders they would weigh so much on my mind as to leave no room for other effective thoughts. . . .

You cannot avoid giving the key of the Bank's safe to the Local Manager. . . . For one risk avoided by liberal provision of extra rule and line a dozen new risks are introduced. Get rid of every manager who shows clear want of common sense, or of power to say no. Let those who are left have as much liberty as may be at all reasonable, proportioned to their experience and proved character.[11]

From an account by a superintendent in The Lincoln Electric Company:

When Mr. Lincoln put me in charge of the electrode division, he . . . merely said that I was responsible to him for the men, the machinery, and the plant, and to our customers for the product; that I should contact him on any problems where I felt his experience would be useful; and that I should keep him informed of anything out of the ordinary that took place. . . .

Three months after I started the job, the machine division moved out to a new plant. With it went the engineering department and all the general offices. The problem under any more formal method of delegation and limitation of authority and responsibility would have

---

11. S. J. Butlin, *Australia and New Zealand Bank* (London and New York: Longmans, Green and Co., 1961), pp. 264-265.

been intolerable. I was isolated in the old plant; and in trying to get on top of my new job, I did not maintain proper liaison with some of the other executives. I made unilateral decisions about things I had not even thought about three months before.

It took about three weeks for the boom to fall. A telephone call started it. Certain charges were extra because of some of my decisions. To which of my accounts did I want to charge them? There were other calls about other charges. A government regulation was violated because of one of my agreements with the people taking over our old building. How did I want to handle it?

I was not bailed out by someone else; I had to cope with the results of my own mistakes myself. Mr. Lincoln never mentioned them. I am sure he was told about them, probably before I was, and I am sure he asked (because he has asked a like question of me in like circumstances), "Have you gone over this with Willis yet?" [12]

In planning work and assigning jobs, the manager assumes that most people have far greater possibilities than he can know. In short, he sees people as people—with potentials and contradictions and destinies and origins too deep, profound, and mysterious for him or any other mortal to understand in full. If he thought he knew exactly what to expect of a man or group of men, he would be looking at them as things, believing that, as he could predict what a machine would do, he could predict what a man would do on the basis of his performance, the results of his psychological tests, and so forth. There was a strong tendency to regard people as things in the school of scientific management that was so popular in the first half of the twentieth century. Some of the personnel and "human relations" movements that sprang up had the same tendency to a lesser degree— one group even stressed terms like "human engineering."

The effect of the managerial mind is to keep the executive or supervisor from ever feeling complacent about an employee's performance. He is perpetually dissatisfied, in a sense—worrying that the organization may be cheating itself by expecting too

12. George E. Willis, "Sharpening Your Own Ability to Delegate and Control," in Edward C. Bursk, ed., *The Management Team* (Cambridge: Harvard University Press, 1954), pp. 216-217.

little. Could a man have given *more* than was expected of him? Because the standard or expectation was set by someone else with authority or influence over him, did he resent it and therefore stop short of his best? Did the expectation limit his thinking because it was based on what he had done in the past that was subject to many frustrations and restrictions? As one top executive I know is used to saying, "No one ever gave his best."

To the extent that expectations are necessary, they are considered more justifiable if high. The logic of this attitude is simple: The higher our expectations of a man on a job, the more leeway we are generally forced to give him in the choice of methods, and the more general and broad our expectations have to be. If I expect my bureau chief to turn in the same record of accomplishment next year that he made last year, I can give him fairly explicit instructions. If, however, because of an emergency or other reasons, I ask him to accomplish far more, I cannot regulate him so closely and must rely more on his willingness to work toward a goal as best *he* thinks he can. The truth of this assumption has been demonstrated often in both wartime and peacetime.

"In business," writes an executive of Owens-Illinois, "a great deal more than reassurance goes into the development of a man. I have heard from Likert's own research staff that, regardless of differing leadership styles, outstanding results rarely if ever come from groups where the leader does not hold up high standards." [13] A college president has noted how high expectations tend to maintain initiative in both parties to a working relationship:

He [the chief executive of an organization] may judge and discipline them [subordinates] when they err, if he has developed for himself sufficiently reliable standards of private judgment. Note, however, that his judgment will consist largely in continuously set-

13. Harold Mayfield, "In Defense of Performance Appraisal," *Harvard Business Review,* March-April, 1960, p. 84. The man referred to is Dr. Rensis Likert of The University of Michigan.

ting before them high standards of excellence with which they cannot fail to compare themselves. Their ability or inability to reach these standards will generally become so apparent to themselves and their colleagues that they will either respond with better effort or resign." [14]

A Mixture of Motives

What are the manager's personal motives in trying to keep expectations from molding and inhibiting his and his associates' thinking?

One motive, obviously, is material gain. If his people continually exceed themselves, he, they, and the organization in general gain in prestige, power, and (in the case of private business) profits.

A second motive is occupational security through the avoidance of stagnation and rigidity. This motive is perhaps most apparent in competitive industry, where the specter of unemployment hovers over the firm that slips behind the leaders. An organization can develop a kind of myopia from expectations, with people paying more attention to fulfilling their expectations of each other than to the fundamental problem of growth and survival in a changing world.

A third motive, I submit, is the desire to project the lesson of personal experience. Most administrators of any importance in government, education, and industry would not be where they are if they hadn't repeatedly surpassed people's expectations of them. They know firsthand what the burden of expectations can do to a person. Having struggled so hard to cast it off in their own lives, they quite naturally struggle against it as a matter of principle wherever it is found. This attitude seems to have been conspicuous in the careers of many military leaders, in particular. Here is a revealing note on General Sheridan of Civil War fame —time, April 1, 1865; place, Five Forks, Virginia:

---

14. Louis W. Norris, "Moral Hazards of an Executive," *Harvard Business Review*, July-August, 1960, p. 77.

The sun was just disappearing over the treetops, and the clearing was dim with smoky twilight. Many soldiers were in and about the road through the clearing, their weapons in their hands, conscious of victory and half expecting to be told that they had done a great thing and were very fine fellows. Sheridan turned to face them, and he suddenly stood up in his stirrups, waving his hat, his face as black as his horse, and in a great voice he roared:

"I want you men to understand we have a record to make before that sun goes down that will make Hell tremble!" [15]

A fourth motive is escape. Ordinarily we think of managers as a hardheaded lot. Corporate treasurers, army colonels, assistant deans—these men are used to the practical realities of human nature and have learned to live with them. Yet they have longings for utopia like everyone else. "Ross's mind," wrote James Thurber of *The New Yorker's* editor, "was always filled with dreams of precision and efficiency beyond attainment, but exciting to contemplate." [16] High expectations are a way of ignoring people's real batting averages on the job and keeping alive the dream of The Perfect Subordinate or The Perfect Work Force. Sometimes—not often, but often enough—the dream almost comes true.

A fifth motive is a kind of "organizational immortality" enhanced by the development of good lieutenants and successors. This motive may be becoming more general in this age, when an organization can, if it is successful, live many years. Some time ago, a manuscript came to the *Harvard Business Review* that I have always remembered even though we were unable to use it at the time. It was a frank statement of personal philosophy by a business leader, and while I cannot remember his exact words I can recall the spirit and general thrust of them. The gist of the message was:

When I was a young man starting out in business I wanted money most of all. In time money came and I began to turn my

---

15. Bruce Catton, *A Stillness at Appomattox* (Garden City: Doubleday & Company, Inc., 1953), p. 357.

16. James Thurber, *The Years With Ross* (Boston: Little, Brown and Company, 1957), p. 8.

sights more to power. I played for high stakes in deadly earnest and was profoundly excited by the game. Then the fascination of the game began to fail. I looked ahead. I looked past my retirement at this business into which I had put the better part of a lifetime of effort. I wondered, "What next? What after me? Will it all go when I go?" I found myself regarding our people in a different light. The plant and books of account that had so long been a personal thing in my mind, a prize to be divided by victors, became instead an institution that must go on. And nothing that our people could do was too good, as far as I was concerned, nor could any hope for them be too high.

IMPLICATIONS FOR INDIVIDUALS

Let us turn once again to the question raised in the introduction. What is the importance of this chapter of *The Managerial Mind* to those considering administration as a career and to those already in administration who want a rationale for their approach to problems?

1. *The new manager will find the individuality and pattern of the managerial mind reinforced by the philosophy of expectations.* The sense of commitment to the organization, the attitudes toward differences and tension are bolstered by these ideas about expectations. The managerial mind not only gains in internal consistency but is also set further apart from other ways of thinking. Note, however, that it is the "people" aspects, rather than the technical aspects of administration that encourage this trend. In his approach to a technical problem like cost analysis or forecasting, the manager can proceed much as any good professional analyst would.

2. *Even the veteran manager cannot hope to routinize his dealings with employees; he must continually improvise.* The attitude about expectations means that the patterned approach to a personnel problem can never be good enough. The element of practiced, professional, creative judgment is indispensable—as

much so in administration as in scientific research. Administration cannot be broken down into neat rules and formulas like a game of bridge; an administrative problem cannot be programed for a computer.

3. *The would-be administrator can be confident that, at least if he develops a managerial mind, his work will be fun.* These ideas about expectations guarantee a large element of suspense, surprise, and excitement. One part of working productively through people involves a kind of gambling that never ends and offers no possibility of the odds ever being lopsided in the bettor's favor.

8

LEVELS

OF

KNOWLEDGE

IN

MANAGERIAL

THINKING

WHAT KINDS OF KNOWLEDGE are important to the administrator? In his needs for information, how is he like and how is he different from people in other professions and vocations?

The answers to these questions will increase our understanding of the managerial mind and help to guide managers and would-be managers in their careers. They will at the same time illuminate one of the most common reasons for underestimating the qualities needed by men and women in administration. For example, there can be no question that, if we compare what the manager needs to know with what the lawyer or doctor needs to know, doing so in terms of the scope of legal or medical knowledge, we will find the manager's needs are smaller. He does not need to know so much, and he does not have to have so much analytical skill in applying it. If we recognize that not one but *several* levels of knowledge are important to the manager, however, and use all of these levels in the comparison, we must reach a quite different conclusion.

The word "level," as I shall use it here, does not imply a hierarchy of values or needs. The first level may well be more fundamental and deeper than the second or third, or *vice versa,* depending on one's point of view and the situation. I use the term "level" simply to indicate differences in texture, structure, use, and origin. The term is also helpful because it suggests proximity. While the levels to be described are different in central emphasis, they tend at the edges and borders to run into each other and intermingle.

METHODS

The first level of knowledge may be called methods or techniques.[1] (Some may prefer to call this level of knowledge problem-solving in the narrow sense of the term.) When the lawyer uses his knowledge of court procedure, judicial precedent, and statutory interpretation to serve a client, he is solving a problem. The physician is engaged in the same kind of activity when he diagnoses a patient's illness and prescribes a treatment. The engineer uses understanding of methods to build a bridge that meets a client's specifications as to load, safety, and appearance. The accountant uses a similar approach when he draws up an

---

1. The existence of this and other levels was suggested by Sir Geoffrey Vickers's article, "Judgment," in *The Manager,* January, 1961.

income statement or balance sheet. The trader, too, uses it when he negotiates a financial deal, sale, or corporate merger.

Similarly, the administrator uses knowledge in problem-solving when he gets a "trouble-shooting" assignment from his boss or meets a crisis in the office. The knowledge may come from written materials, conversations, observation, or past experience.

Generally speaking, such knowledge is brought to bear when a specific task is assigned or made necessary by events, that is, when the situation to be worked out comes to the manager more or less ready-made, and his job is to reach a solution if he can. Part of his skill may be used in sizing up the problem or recognizing that there is a problem, but essentially his work is laid out for him.

Much of the material in textbooks on administration today is knowledge about methods. Much of the instruction in management-training programs also deals with such information.

Illustrations. What are some specific kinds of problem-solving or methods information valued by administrators? A few examples follow:

Most of our knowledge about production scheduling, work flow, plant layout, machine design, and other aspects of modern production is in this category.

Our knowledge about how to plan the size of inventories and "couple" them efficiently with sales and production is a good example of problem-solving knowledge.

In the Federal Bureau of Old-Age Survivors & Disability Insurance, supervisors have reportedly saved American taxpayers millions of dollars by suggesting modifications to the punch card and to the electronic process by which Social Security records are kept. These efforts called for problem-solving knowledge (of data-processing techniques, organizational behavior, time study, and so forth).

A company found itself losing more and more business to competitors; both production and sales costs rose to dangerous levels. Applying techniques of market research, it was able to ascertain why old customers were leaving and where its most profitable opportunities in the market lay. These techniques were an example of methods knowledge.

Comparisons. Most vocations make strong demands on problem-solving knowledge. To take an extreme example, a mechanic uses almost nothing but this form of information when he fixes a machine. Nearly all professions require it too. A good military officer should have a great deal of such information, especially in directing combat. A man who makes his living buying and selling goods for profit needs to know much about the tactics of skillful trading.

While information about techniques is vital to the manager, as the proliferation of university courses, books, and organizational training programs suggests, it may well be even more important to the lawyer, doctor, engineer, and certain other professionals. Their requirements may exceed the manager's in this respect.

Significance. One outstanding aspect of this type of knowledge is that it is important in all ranks of administration—from the supervisor to the president in a corporation, from the office manager to the chairman in a government agency, from an administrative assistant to the president or chancellor in a university. It is also clear that most managers spend a large proportion of their time using information of this variety. Indeed, there seems to be a growing opinion among management experts that too *much* time is spent this way, especially at the middle and higher levels of authority. Such information is basic, however. Without it, the other levels of data to be discussed would be meaningless.

A person's ability to retain and apply problem-solving data can probably be measured with fair success by intelligence and proficiency tests. When the late Professor Benjamin M. Selekman used to argue with colleagues that men in medicine and science were, on the average, "brighter" than men in management, he was comparing them in terms of the kinds of skill and aptitude measured by most academic tests. As we shall see presently, however, other levels call for abilities that are not so readily evaluated.

Finally, it should be mentioned that the manager's dependence on methods knowledge does not set him apart from men in other fields. In this respect, at least, he is more *like* most professionals than different from them.

REALITY

The second level of knowledge important to the managerial mind might be called information about reality, about the environment. The concern here is with the world around the organization—people, conditions, trends. What are a group of people really arguing about? What is the real profit condition of the company? Is government becoming more hostile to business or not? Such questions call on knowledge of and ability to judge the realities of a situation. Much of the space in magazines today is devoted to describing and interpreting such realities.

The division between this level of knowledge and the other levels is not always distinct. For instance, market researchers in business often interweave both reality and problem-solving knowledge—for example, when the assignment is to ascertain which are the most profitable parts of the company's business (reality knowledge) and to indicate how much the firm can increase its earnings by marketing more skillfully for those segments (problem-solving level).

Illustrations. Here are some examples of the use of reality knowledge in different fields of administration:

The efforts of various government agencies and commissions to assess economic conditions in this country—and of intelligence organizations to assess political and military situations abroad—fall at this level.

A college administration's attempt to start a fund-raising drive at the opportune moment stimulates efforts to collect reality knowledge—for instance, estimates of when prospective donors are likely to be in a receptive frame of mind, undistracted by tax deadlines, other fund drives, and bad publicity.

Business forecasting data are a clear case of environmental knowledge.

The managers of a food company operating in a foreign country found that more and more of the firm's sales were going through chain warehouses rather than company warehouses, as had traditionally been the case. As a result, management gave up much of its high investment in a private distribution system, counting largely on sales through the chain centers instead. This decision was based on reality knowledge.

One of the country's pioneers in discount stores is well-known for delegating almost all his paper work to others so that he can spend his time on the selling floor watching customers shop, observing their reactions, talking with clerks and buyers, and so forth. Since he is highly dependent on accurate assessments of buying trends, he is keenly interested in acquiring reality knowledge.

Early in the 1950's, executives of General Electric Company, Lockheed Aircraft, and a number of other corporations began selling the idea to their managements that a vigorous United States defense effort was here to stay and that their firms should gear their plans to that outlook. In making such assessments, they were dealing with knowledge at the reality level.

Comparisons. While reality knowledge ranks in significance with problem-solving knowledge in the managerial mind, in many occupations this level is not so important as the first. In some of the applied sciences, for example, men are not likely to have the vital stake in assessing trends and conditions that the policy-making manager does. On the other hand, educators, journalists, and financial analysts count heavily indeed on such assessments.

Significance. This level of information should add to our appreciation of the scope of the managerial mind. We see that it can no longer properly be compared with other "minds" on the basis of only one kind of requirement for knowledge. The picture becomes broader.

Intelligence and proficiency tests seem to be poor measures of facility with this kind of information; the questions normally included in an intelligence test usually involve vocabulary, sentence completion, arithmetic, analogies, reasoning problems, and others that emphasize academic know-how more than reality judgments. It is necessary to look more closely at the performance record and count more heavily on intuitive judgments when evaluating one's knowledge at this level. A complicating factor in our judgments of one person's facility with reality knowledge is that what we accept as reality depends partly on his (or possibly someone else's) ability to *persuade* us to his view. Our judgments must be more subjective. At the problem-solving level, by contrast, the correctness of a solution is more readily tested.

Knowledge of the environment is probably more important at the middle and upper ranks of an organization's management than in the lowest ones because more policy-making for the department or company as a whole is contributed by the former. The organization can, however, still be a small one or part of a larger one. For example, the heads of a quality control section may be no less intimately concerned with environmental knowledge than are the heads of the whole corporation, although the information pertinent to their interests is, of course, of a different nature—relations with other departments, top management's interest in quality control, and so forth.

It is worth noting that when management leaders like Clarence Randall, former head of Inland Steel, have asked for more allocation of time from paper work for the sake of reflection, they have had men in the upper ranks primarily in mind.

Finally, the value of environmental knowledge has been increasing in recent years as a result of greater emphasis on broad "systems thinking"; that is, conceiving of the organization as a system acting on and reacting to conditions in the environment.

This trend in thought has naturally shifted more and more attention to the organization's relations with the community, the markets, other organizations, and the economy.

DESIRABLE GOALS

A third level of knowledge has to do with what managers *want* to happen, conditions they *desire,* goals they *seek.* Here we are in the realm of values. Analytical thinking plays a supporting role to insight, imagination, vision.

Great leaders have typically excelled at this level, but it is by no means their exclusive domain. Liberal-arts courses in college deal with it, as do many magazine articles and books. As private individuals and citizens, we all think and talk about ideas and information dealing with what we want for the future.

This level of information is radically different from the other two and especially from the first—in substance, in nature, in its demands on the individual, in its impact on operations. Its importance is beyond dispute. The history of organizational life can make little sense if we leave out this factor, for time and again managers have set courses bearing little relation to their knowledge of realities or techniques but a strong relation indeed to their views of what was desirable for the operation.

To be sure, this level of information is not knowledge in as strict or formal a sense as the problem-solving and reality varieties. It is interwoven with assumptions, values, imaginative insights, and ideals. In the final analysis, however, all these elements can be traced back to observation, information heard and read, associations of ideas, parental influence, and so forth. Not all of this stream of experience can fairly be called knowledge, especially accurate knowledge, but some of it can. Perhaps the most significant difference is that its validity and correctness are not so easily tested as information at the other levels. It is not necessarily so "factual" in nature.

Illustrations. How does information at this level show up in administrative action? Here are a few illustrations:

In one midwestern company, a manager decided that the climate of supervision in his department was too rigid, authoritarian, and controlled. He revamped his thinking and began working for policies of looser supervision, less regimentation, more individual freedom to experiment and deviate from the "rule book." This decision was based on third-level knowledge gained from talking, observing, and reading about desirable patterns of supervision.

The executives of a labor union took the position that their organization should do more to preserve and further the long-range profit position of the company. Their decision was based on information about the policies certain other unions had found desirable, on notions about the amount of work that could and should exist in the area if manufacturing developed locally instead of moving away, on general ideas about the proper role of organized labor, and similar matters.

Henry Ford was drawing on ideas and fragments of information at the third level when he set his pioneering policies regarding car prices and workers' pay—for instance, that it would be desirable to make a car that every family could own and that wages should be set at a higher rate than they had been prior to the 1920's.

Gifford Pinchot, the great conservationist, used knowledge of what is desirable for society when he convinced the country of the need for federal policies to preserve forests, wild life, and other natural resources. Not facts so much as information about *ideas* was what influenced him.

Some years ago, a large corporation was plagued with law suits for damage to employees' health resulting from conditions in the foundries. The chief executive, after pondering these claims, decided the company should thereafter go far beyond the minimum standards of health and safety in work areas, not because it had to but because that was the "right" thing to do. By contrast, problem-solving knowledge would probably have led him to urge more preventive legal measures.

Alfred Sloan's dedication to the concept of systematic, departmentalized, functionalized organization for General Motors (in contrast to the unpatterned, more chaotic system used by Durant) was a reflection in part of knowledge at the third level. The company had not previously practiced the concepts Sloan wanted; they were truly innovative. Yet they were based on a good deal of information about organizational patterns that others had espoused in the past and that impressed him as desirable, too.

Comparisons. While knowledge at the third level is vital to the thoughtful manager in policy making—without it he cannot effectively set new directions and standards for the organization—it is not nearly so important to people in most professions and vocations. The accountant has little need of it. The engineer does not use it very much in his work; he must accept the properties of various materials and designs as they are and usually he must accept his client's wishes. The doctor treats the human body as it is, not as he might wish it to be. The legal mind, too, takes the law "as is," although lawyers may complain about it privately and politically. As a matter of fact, judges have often been careful to point out in their decisions that their function is to apply the law and to interpret the intent of legislatures, not to consider what the statutes should be.

On the other hand, knowledge of what is desirable is highly important to such groups as political leaders and teachers. The managerial point of view is not the only one in which this level of knowledge plays a key role.

Significance. Goals knowledge is more important to managers in policy-making positions than in the first ranks of supervision. Aside from this distinction, however, its value is fairly constant in the administrative mind. In small organizations as well as in large, in departments and divisions of large complexes as well as in headquarters offices, information at this level is of continuing interest and importance. In a production department in one plant of a great corporation, questions about the kind of work that should be done and the kinds of supervisory policy that should be followed may come up as often as in the president's office of a small business—although the freedom of decision may naturally be more circumscribed.

Intelligence and related tests of analytical ability are not useful in evaluating facility with knowledge at this level. To evaluate a man's capacity to absorb and use this kind of information, we are forced more than ever to use intuition and the performance record as our guides. What is more, so much depends on what we are *persuaded* is a proper goal.

This level of knowledge should add greatly to our appreciation of the depth of the managerial mind. Not only does it take us into dark reaches of information beyond the limits of most professional and vocational thinking, but it suggests that the intellectual requirements of administration might compare quite favorably with the requirements of the established professions if we only had a good measure of ability to absorb and manipulate goals knowledge.

Finally, to emphasize an earlier point, the manager's use of knowledge at this level affects his needs at the other levels. For example, he decides the kinds of human-relations problems with which he will wrestle when he decides what policies of delegation and supervision he wants—perhaps whether he will concentrate more on relations among people than on details of individuals' work. He decides the number and nature of customer complaints he will contend with when he decides what level of service to maintain for customers of a certain product. If a marketing executive decides that his department should be greatly concerned with the question of what businesses the company should be in he makes it essential to learn about problems and realities that would be outside his bailiwick if he were concentrating only on the efficiency of the current marketing effort.

IMPLICATIONS FOR INDIVIDUALS

For practitioners and would-be practitioners of management, these levels of knowledge have a number of implications.

1. *Students should not underestimate the needs for knowledge in administration by assuming, as we so often have done in the past, that any single type of information is the key to understanding.* A true perspective takes in at least three levels of knowledge.

2. *Capacity to manipulate knowledge at the different levels may vary greatly among equally "intelligent" people.* Ability at the different levels is even likely to vary greatly during the course of a single career. There is thus another dimension to the problem of matching people to jobs. Some jobs in organizations obviously call for a good deal more in the way of methods information than other jobs do, and some positions call for more knowledge and experience with values and goals.

3. *The quality of executive judgment is related to facility with knowledge at the different levels.* For example, determination of the way to analyze a financial problem hinges on experience with past problems and knowledge of methods (first level). Again, skill in judging market conditions depends partly on general knowledge and experience with appraisals of the market (second level).

4. *The ability to persuade is more important with knowledge at the third level than with problem-solving data.* This difference exists because what other people *accept* as valid reasoning depends more on whether or not they happen to share the general point of view of the communicator. By contrast, the ability to analyze, dissect, and test would seem to be more important when applying problem-solving knowledge, where the correctness of a solution can be demonstrated more objectively. The middle level—reality knowledge—appears to call for a blend of the two abilities.

5. *A man advancing in management should find value in kinds of preparation other than formal training programs.* For instance, knowledge of what is desirable may be gained effectively through reading, informal talks, and reflection. University courses, in-plant training sessions, and other organized programs may kindle interest and help test goals thinking, but the creative seed can grow without a classroom. On the other hand, the stimulus of formal assignments and organized discussion seem to be less dispensable in learning how to use methods or problem-solving knowledge.

9

TEACHING

AND

THE

MANAGERIAL

MIND

TEACHING IS IMPORTANT to the manager because it underlies the chances for success of almost everything he tries to do for the organization. Much of his knowledge is useless if he cannot pass it on to others. Furthermore, most principles or techniques of organization—chain of command, goal-setting, delegation, control, and so forth—are of little avail to him if he can't teach effectively. Conversely, if he *can* teach, he can break almost any rule in a manual or text and still get a good deal of work done successfully through others.

(141)

Few values distinguish the administrative mind from other "minds" as clearly as does the importance attached to teaching. Of all the professions and vocations, only professional teaching itself is so dependent on the ability to transmit knowledge and understanding to others. Within the ranks of organizational authority, no function so sharply separates manager from non-manager as does teaching.

To illustrate this point I draw on an example described by Charles A. Nelson.[1] A shoemaker, writes Nelson, has a practical knowledge of leather and shoes. He uses this knowledge to shape the shoe according to a pattern in his mind or on a paper before him. As long as his business is making shoes by hand, it is enough if his personal knowledge and manual skills can be combined to please customers. If he becomes an entrepreneur, however, he must hire a number of men with various degrees of skill to make shoes under his direction. Not all of them will know enough about the trade, and those who do may have different standards from his own.

How is he to transmit the necessary knowledge and skill? He can describe the job, he can write out instructions, he can demonstrate, and he can devise other methods. In performing any of these activities, Nelson points out, he teaches. "A manager or foreman may be many things, but he must be a teacher . . . it is perfectly possible to have a completely knowledgeable man who is a poor teacher because, while he has knowledge of the subject and even a theoretical knowledge of men and how they learn, he may not have developed the art of combining the knowledge and transmitting it successfully to others."

Now let us suppose that the shoemaker builds a factory and hires foremen to assist him in supervising the workers. He has not only operators under him but other managers. He must instruct the latter how to tell men how to make shoes as he used to make them. He must be able to teach men not only how to use the

1. Charles A. Nelson, "The Liberal Arts in Management," *Harvard Business Review*, May-June, 1958, pp. 94-95.

equipment but how to teach what they know to others. He "is more and more concerned with men and less and less with shoes."

If our shoemaker does not come to see his job in this way but continues to think as he did when he was making the shoes himself, his organization is doomed to rigidity and stagnation. Managers are familiar enough with this principle from personal experience, for almost every organization has had some contact with bosses who could not teach. There is also much documentary evidence. One study covers a medium-sized supermarket chain in which several important moves in the direction of decentralization have been initiated by top management.[2] Some of the district and store managers are able to take on the added functions that headquarters has assigned to them, but one district manager and his store manager are slow in making progress. It appears that this district manager has been in the habit of telling his store manager exactly what he wants done. Even in smallest details of display and storage, he has guided the subordinate, rather than teaching him store management. In consequence, the store manager is afraid to do anything that his boss has not specifically instructed and therefore fails to take initiative or to be aggressive. The two men together have fallen behind the other teams in handling the new, expanded role that top management wants local managers to take on. The district manager's inability to teach has thus jeopardized his very existence as a manager.

PREFERRED PATTERNS

What kinds of teaching are considered most important in the administrator's view? Why are they valued?

---

2. Paul R. Lawrence, *The Changing of Organizational Behavior Patterns* (Boston: Division of Research, Harvard Business School, 1958), pp. 115-128.

Personal example. Several years ago, I spent some time talking with executives of a large industrial manufacturing firm about what they had learned from their bosses and how. This firm was an especially interesting one to study because there was practically no teaching device that headquarters hadn't tried. It appeared certain that the speeches and articles of senior officers at headquarters had been helpful. It appeared, too, that some training programs had made a contribution. The most profound impact, however, seemed to have come from the personal examples of managers. The subordinates did not always recognize consciously how much they had been taught in this way, and often the bosses had not intended their actions to be instructive. Yet repeatedly it was what the boss had actually *done* in hiring, firing, promoting, delegating, that turned out to have made the most impression on an assistant. Impressions conveyed in this way, it seems to me, become an important part of executive thinking.

What things are best taught by personal example? Management methods are a good "subject." When a subordinate sees his boss act in certain ways and witnesses results as well, he may learn much about the method. A more important "subject" is attitudes, values, and philosophies. For example, when a company is "down and out," how can a manager stimulate an aggressive, never-say-die spirit effectively *except* by personal example? A book, a study program, a memo may be pallid teachers indeed when an organization is in the grip of defeatism and despair. The sharp, hard experience of working with an enthusiastic leader may develop attitudes with tremendous power. A case in point is an episode from the history of Goodyear Tire & Rubber Company, when as a smaller firm it was plagued by depression worries, sinking morale, and the psychology of retreat. The production manager (later president) tells his story:

> I do recall standing at my office window looking out into space, as I often do when I have something on my mind, and becoming conscious that Eddie Thomas [secretary] was at my elbow.

"You are to talk to the branch managers at ten o'clock," he said when he got my attention. "Here are your notes."

I stared at him a minute without realizing what he was saying. Then I stuffed the notes in my pocket, went over to the meeting. . . . I did not talk about the things a factory man ordinarily discusses with salesmen. I know too that I did not mince words. If this cost my job, so be it.

"Up to now this company has been retreating," I said. "That was necessary. But we've reached the point now, like Sheridan at Winchester, where we've got to quit retreating and start fighting. We've got to stop thinking about saving money and start thinking about *making* money. We can't pay off our debts by cutting expenses. We can only do that by going out after business and getting it. We've lost a lot of money, but that isn't important as long as we haven't lost the fighting spirit that built this company.

"We have plenty of weapons to fight with," I reminded them. "The biggest one is our reputation. Our friends are sticking with us, General Motors, Ford, Nash, and the rest at Detroit, and our dealers all over the country. They have gone through the fire too. The public is for us. They have found out that year after year Goodyear has given them the best damned tire in the world.

"This company was not built by ordinary men using ordinary methods," I concluded. "It was built by thoroughbreds who outstripped their competitors in sales, production, development, engineering, and everything else. We can do it again. It will take hard work, courage, drive, determination. But no one is ever licked until he admits he is. You men are still thoroughbreds. Let's start fighting."

I must have talked for half an hour, so intent was I on my theme. As I finished a surprising thing happened. Every man in the room was up on his feet cheering, and kept on cheering, then started scrambling up on the platform. Wilmer, the president, was the first one. He had a smile on his face and his hand was outstretched.

"I see what you mean, Litch," he said, "and I am with you 100 per cent."[3]

The exact words and sequence of points used by Litchfield that morning were probably soon forgotten by most of his

3. P. W. Litchfield, *Industrial Voyage* (New York: Doubleday & Company, Inc., 1954), pp. 204-205.

listeners, but the attitude he demonstrated helped to teach the work force that it was never too late to start a comeback. It should not be surprising that this form of teaching—itself often learned by personal example—ranks high in importance in the managerial mind.

Discerning questions. A second and highly valued way of teaching is raising questions. The manager finds this method particularly effective if the questions are used, not to manipulate opinion by suggesting certain answers, but to call attention to problems that need to be thought through more forcefully. Many executives value good questions above good answers in teaching managers how to manage; they find that answers are more important only where staff specialists, technicians, and other non-managers are concerned.

In the case of the supermarket chain discussed earlier, one of the district manager-store manager teams was remarkably effective in taking on the new responsibilities. The district manager saw that personnel development was a key problem, and the following brief excerpt from one of many routine conversations will suggest how he put his point across—in this instance, to the store's meat manager:

"How's your head cutter coming along?"
"Well, he's coming along fine, I think he's really doing well."
"Do you think he'd do as well if he were under a new manager all of a sudden?"
"Well, I don't know, I think so."
"Do you think he's ready to go out on his own yet?"
"Well, I don't think he is yet. But I think if you give him six months he will. He's certainly got all the brains that anybody needs to do this, and I think about six months' more experience and he'll be in good shape."
"Well, that's the way to do it. . . . " [4]

Note that the district manager is not telling the meat manager what to do about his head cutter. He is not suggesting that the cutter is ready or not ready to go out on his own; he is only

---

4. Lawrence, *op. cit.,* p. 85.

teaching the importance of personnel development to the meat manager by making it the chief point of his questions.

This example suggests that the discerning question is more useful in communicating values than in communicating facts, formulas, or techniques. It is useful in teaching the elements of the managerial mind itself, for the managerial mind, as this book shows, is better defined by the values it professes than by the methods it emphasizes. For instance, a marketing manager may teach a department head to think of the organization as an organic whole by asking him questions like, "How can we make closer ties between ourselves and our channels of distribution?" To teach a production manager the importance of differences as described in Chapter 3, a plant manager might ask, "How many different kinds of foreman do we need to cover the variety of problems we have?" To teach an assistant the importance of looking aggressively for problems as described in Chapter 5, a credit manager may ask, "What are the three most troublesome complaints concerning our credit policies for new customers?"

Planning. It may at first seem strange to list planning as a teaching device. Usually we think of planning in terms of goals and programs for attaining them—a kind of ladder into the future, more the result of knowledge than a means to knowledge. Actually, however, planning's value as a strategic weapon is only a little greater than its value in instruction. Why does the manager reason this way?

First, planning is helpful in teaching the vital "subject" of standards. In discussions with associates, the manager continually hears expressions like "sound financing," "broad appeal," "safer course," and "good research." Such words seem inevitable when men talk about an uncertain future. Their occurrence affords an unusual opportunity to analyze the meaning of men's experience and concepts. What do we mean by *sound* financing? How broad is a *broad* appeal? What are the most important risks to guard against in mapping a *safer* course? What does past experience tell us about criteria for *good* research?

Second, the planning process is calculated to develop fresh knowledge about the environment of the organization—new trends, future problems, and so forth. Military planning may lead to new intelligence about the status of the prospective enemy's armaments, business planning to fresh research on consumers' needs and desires, educational planning to more authoritative data on the changing school population. This knowledge frequently can be produced only through planning. Moreover, it is produced at a time when men are ready for it. The problem has been on their minds, if the planning has been done intelligently and with good communications, and they are in a receptive mood for learning. The teacher could hardly ask for better stage setting.

Third, the manager finds planning helpful in discovering and transmitting knowledge of the capabilities of the organization. Men stand back from the immediate task and try to take an objective look at their strengths and weaknesses. Data and opinions from different parts of the organization are drawn together and assembled, often with surprising results to all concerned. If an intelligent planning approach has been taken, the knowledge becomes available at a time when employees have been made curious about it.

Each of these uses of planning in teaching is helpful. Together, however, they may be more than that. They may be so essential that management cannot continue without them. A case once described by Henry Bund of the Research Institute of America, Inc., serves to illustrate my point.[5] The company was a medium-sized manufacturer of consumer durables. It had its own sales force selling to wholesalers. Volume was reasonably good, but profits were shrinking, and there was cause for alarm. Bund's description implies that the firm had a competent staff of em-

_____

5.   Henry Bund, "Steps in Successful Marketing Planning," in David W. Ewing, ed., *Effective Marketing Action* (New York: Harper & Brothers, 1958), pp. 303-307.

ployees and that management was probably teaching by some of the means available to it but not by planning.

One morning, the president came into his office and found a special-delivery letter. Here is Bund's disguised version of the letter:

Dear Mr. Hackett:

Four months ago I purchased one of your products from the Easy Retailing Company here in town. It looked like a dandy and for two months it worked fine. Then it stopped. The company sent out a service man, and as it was Saturday and I was home, I watched him work. After only a few minutes it was apparent that he was not sure what he was doing. However, he finally decided that the trouble was in one particular part and that it would have to be replaced. I asked him if we would be able to use the machine on Sunday. He said that he did not think so because they had been unable to get any parts. That was two months ago, and the damned thing is not fixed yet. Unfortunately, I paid cash. What do I do now?

Sincerely,

Bert Blister.

This letter touched off a chain reaction, Bund reports. The president found out that there were plenty of open orders for parts but that order service could not get them from production. Production in turn said that it could not get anticipated failure rates from the engineers. The engineers said they were waiting for field experience. The problem was going round and round with nothing being done.

In establishing a strong marketing department and instituting planning, one of the first things the president emphasized was the importance of standards. The level of customer service was not good enough; it had to be improved. The prevailing committee system had apparently not been able to teach its importance. Valuable knowledge about the competitive environment was also gained. Under the planning approach, executives went out and determined the size and location of markets, trends in competition, service requirements, approximate price, and so forth. They then furnished this information to engineering, manufacturing, and cost-analysis executives. Their *attitude* toward marketing began to change.

Finally, managers found it possible to investigate and test the strengths and weaknesses of the corporate set-up with more understanding than before. To take but one illustration, preparations for good customer service were begun early. Service and parts personnel knew that by a given date certain information about parts and stocks must be in dealers' hands. Knowing how long it would take to print that information, they worked backward to set a date for receiving it in usable form. After agreeing with the engineering department on how long it would take to prepare the data, they worked backward again and set a deadline for furnishing drawings. This general procedure was carried out in various stages and groups, with the result that a complete plan finally emerged. Then, when the plan began to be implemented, progress was charted against the dates on the program. Through the negotiations and data collection thus involved, the staff was able to reach a new level of understanding of what different groups could do, how fast, and with what limitations.

Bund's case demonstrates all three of the teaching values of planning—knowledge about standards, the environment, and internal capabilities. The possibility seems real that without the pressure and motivation of planning, executives would have been able neither to teach nor to learn what it was necessary to know in order to keep the organization going. Perhaps this kind of experience was in one executive's mind when he told me that "Nine tenths of the value of planning is in the planning, not in the program that results."

The "big picture." Fourth, the administrator teaches by pointing out the interrelationships of people, groups, and departments. He considers this kind of teaching important because it helps to transmit an understanding of the needs of the whole organization, as contrasted to the needs of special-interest groups.

He thus infuses those around him with the same sense of commitment to the organization that he feels.

How, specifically, does he do it? He may use a simple, personal approach, perhaps a tactful warning to an over-enthusiastic assistant not to volunteer so many extra services on an outgoing order because the customer may come to expect the "extras" on future orders that will be handled by less able men. The "big picture" may also be taught at the policy level when major interests come into conflict. In the Wilshire Shoe Company case, for instance, there was a dispute over wage rates. The firm was in a rural area and paying less for some jobs than it would have paid had it been in the city. The union business agent came to the company president arguing for "equal pay for equal work." On the surface, his case was a good one, but the president refused to buy it. He had a view of his own:

BUSINESS AGENT: We should get the city rates here, because our membership pays the same dues in both places and should get the same pay for the same work.

COMPANY PRESIDENT: Have you checked how many jobs here pay more than the city rates? I know we have some. Our wage structure isn't what it should be, I'll admit, but I've urged you union people to join me in a real job-evaluation or wage-classification program, so that we do the fair thing for everyone, not just for a few people who happen to kick the most. Maybe some of our rates ought to be raised and some ought to be reduced. But we can't keep on making a few increases here, and a few more increases there, and expect to stay in business.[6]

In worrying about the effect of piecemeal increases on the total wage structure, this executive was showing concern for the organization as a system. When operators in one department worked hard and were well paid, he wanted the plant as a whole to gain. He did not want operators in other departments to become so angered by unfair differences in pay checks that they would lay down on the job.

---

6. Paul Pigors and Charles A. Myers, *Personal Administration* (3rd ed., New York: McGraw-Hill Book Company, Inc., 1956), pp. 545-546.

Images and aspirations. Finally, the administrator considers it important to teach by creating persuasive images of the future. The officer of a discouraged, poorly equipped, inexperienced military unit paints a vision for his men of the strong, efficient organization they will someday become. The new head of a government office demoralized by a predecessor's graft and laxity describes the prestige and opportunities that will follow development of high standards. Some examples of this type have made history. In the swampy delta of the Orinoco, Simón Bolívar once announced to a few ragged followers that he had just founded the Republic of Gran Colombia and had fixed its capital at Bogotá, a thousand miles away across the Andes. Franklin Roosevelt painted images in his famous "fear" speech; Winston Churchill painted them in his historic "blood, sweat, toil and tears" pledge.

I have called this activity "teaching." Why? What knowledge is conveyed? Persuasive images of the future consist of knowledge of what is desirable and possible. The first involves value judgment, the second reality judgment. Only the manager is likely to be in a position to combine the two. He can make the value judgment because his preoccupation is with people rather than with specialties or products. He can make the reality judgment because his vantage point allows him to see the organization whole—the capabilities of the complete group that he manages as well as conditions outside that affect it. If he is a department supervisor, he is the only one who, in addition to being concerned about the whole department, regularly meets with managers of other departments and can see changes coming in his department's relations with the rest of the company. If he manages a sales organization, he is the one who sees *all* the reports that come in from salesmen.

Only managers could have seen the possibilities of achieving Ford Motor Company's "impossible" dream of production of more than 10,000 cars a day in the 1920's. When the dream was translated into specific steps and goals, the men knew they could meet the challenge and were excited by it:

Men actually worked until they dropped in front of their machines trying to contribute to it. This was on both the Model A and the Model T. . . . There was actually a feeling of exultation when a certain goal was reached on time, and this was prevalent among large numbers of men . . . Men would go over to the superintendent's office and look at the chart showing the production of the day before, and you would see them at quitting time looking at it. Every time ten more motors were added, they would come back and some of them would say, "Come on, boys, tomorrow we will do better." [7]

RELATION TO OTHER ATTITUDES

How does the importance attached to teaching relate to the other values and attitudes of the managerial mind? Let us take them in the order they have been described here.

First, we examined the deep feeling of commitment that the manager feels to his organization. Without this commitment, teaching as the administrator thinks of it would be unimportant, since the function of such teaching is to advance the organization.

Next we examined certain problems and dilemmas revolving around the tendency of direction and control to reduce subordinates' effectiveness. Teaching is related to these concerns because it is a means of developing the abilities of others without making them dependent on the teacher or turning them into mere "extensions" of his personality. None of the five teaching methods outlined, it should be noted, calls for subordinates to memorize answers or to return the same information that is given them.

Then we considered the value placed on differences. Teaching is a way of developing these differences, of making them more significant and meaningful. There would be little need for teaching in an organization where employees are all alike. Of the dif-

---

7. W. A. Nelson, quoted in Allan Nevins and Frank Ernest Hill, *Ford: Expansion and Challenge, 1915-1933* (New York: Charles Scribner's Sons, 1957), pp. 525-526.

ferent methods that help to bring out differences, the second—discerning questions—is probably the most useful, because the subordinate reacts to questions in terms of his own needs, desires, and experience.

As for the importance attached to tension, teaching itself creates tension. As there is tension in the classroom when an instructor is trying to introduce new ways of thinking about a problem or new ideas, so is there added tension in an organization that is being prodded to adapt, adjust, learn, create. An especially good example is the fourth method described: seeking to convey a keener understanding of the interrelationships among individuals and groups. The heart of this teaching method is putting employees into creative opposition with one another—"wind in the sails," to refer back to the analogy.

The next attitude considered was the manager's interest in seeking out problems and turning them to constructive use. Several teaching techniques have obvious value here. For example, planning is likely to force problems into the open that might otherwise have remained concealed, and the questioning technique is helpful in maintaining an aggressive attitude toward problems and failures.

How does teaching bear on the administrator's distrust of manipulation? It is possibly the most effective approach to freeing him from the necessity of completely controlling employee behavior. If he can teach them their trade—or teach others how to teach them—and if he can instruct them in the importance of certain work attitudes and goals, he can turn over to them increasingly large chunks of responsibility. Personal example is particularly important here. Work books, manuals, and technical training have obvious merit in transmitting knowledge of a trade but are of little or no value in helping men relate themselves to their work. Learning of this second type comes from watching and hearing about how the boss "goes at it." Such learning may come slowly, even under the best of circumstances, for it is

checked and channeled and perhaps even distorted by other experiences; but that it comes surely—and often pervasively—no
one can deny.

As for an administrator's expectations of his people, they
could not be so high or flexible but for teaching. To be sure, if
the only way of instruction were by manual and lecture, the
administrator might know exactly what to expect of a man, and
his expectation would not restrict the man. But the teaching
methods most highly valued—personal example, discerning questions, and so forth—work in more subtle, less visible ways, with
the result that the manager is never justified in saying to himself,
"I know exactly what that man's capabilities are." In fact, the
more successful his teaching, the less he is able to know what new
potentials a person may have developed or what new feats he
may be capable of. The use of persuasive images is an especially
valuable teaching technique in this connection because it helps an
organization to keep its sights high and not to underestimate itself.

Timely Growth

In sum, we are justified in making a prediction about this
concept of teaching: Of all the values of the managerial mind,
it is the one most likely to expand and intensify in importance in
the years ahead. In the past, a good deal of the emphasis in
teaching had to be on technical skills. In the case of our shoemaker, for example, he was likely to devote considerable time to
instructing men in the skills of cutting leather, running the
machines, sewing, and finishing. But today—and even more tomorrow—methods training need no longer absorb so much of his
teaching time. He has audio-visual aids, programed instruction,
and even teaching machines to help him with that task. He is
therefore able to devote more time to teaching problem-solving
skills, values, general attitudes.

The old saying that spring comes when it is most needed may well be applicable here. As trends in technology, economics, and population growth have made people increasingly interdependent, the problems of effective organization in industry, education, and government have grown enormously. The big issues have less and less to do with techniques of work and more and more to do with the purposes of work, co-ordination of work, standards, creativity, and equity. These subjects cry loudest for the manager's attention and he has been freed just in time to "teach" at greater length.

IMPLICATIONS FOR INDIVIDUALS

What are the implications of this need for teaching for those looking critically at administration as a career and comparing it with other careers?

1. *The administrator is more like a teacher by the case method than a teacher by the lecture method.* While a good teacher by the case method moderates, suggests, questions, and paraphrases, it is his pupils who do most of the acting, talking, and "showing." He is more in the background, more anonymous than is a teacher by the lecture method. The latter monopolizes the spotlight. In fields where technical methods and know-how are the main thing, the lecturer type might do well enough—but not in administrative operations. Here there are too many values and attitudes to communicate, and wisdom, as Charles Gragg once said, "can't be told."

2. *The new manager will find it important in his field, as in all professions, to have rigorous standards of satisfactory performance.* It must be possible for teacher and "pupil" alike to regard their subject matter with some objectivity.

3. *The value attached to teaching gives the veteran administrator added reason for believing that there is a unique, self-*

reinforcing pattern in his intellectual approach to problems at work. There may indeed be a good deal of "art" in management that is difficult to analyze and to communicate. Yet the demands of the situation are such that knowledge and skills must be passed on as fully as possible. It may be true that the administrator can leave less of this burden to the colleges than can professional men in law, medicine, science, and other fields—that he must do more of the job himself. If so, it only testifies to the great personal importance of teaching as a value in the managerial mind. Teaching helps keep the other qualities of mind alive, and they in turn stimulate the need for teaching.

10

THE

IMPACT

OF

THE

MANAGERIAL

MIND

How DOES ONE TELL whether or not an executive or supervisor has a managerial mind? What visible differences result from the values, attitudes, and assumptions described in previous chapters? The answer to these questions is significant for the light it sheds on the nature of the managerial point of view itself as well as on the problems of management appraisal, organizational policy, and other practical matters.

In general, the way to tell a manager is to look at the behavior of people around him. What are they encouraged to do—and not to do—because of their relationship with him? There are, it seems to me, nine types of reaction to look for. The effects are not necessarily clear-cut or dramatic, but they are more pronounced as a result of the administrator's thinking. While no one or two of them are of decisive importance, taken all together they can provide a "profile" of the executive's influence.

It should be noted in advance that none of the effects to be discussed has to do with how well individuals in the organization like the manager personally or want to emulate him. This discussion also conspicuously omits such criteria as number of employees supervised, size of budget, profit or loss, and prestige because such measures may reflect too many factors other than the quality of management: the efforts of predecessors, luck, accidents of timing, acumen, and various other forces in the organization or field of work. In other words, the managerial mind is but one part of the general problem of over-all organizational effectiveness.

Employees feel more confident. The shy person is a little less shy. The apologetic person gains a little more assurance. The hesitant person feels a little less awkward.

The executive world offers many examples of men with very positive and negative influences in this respect. In one department, the supervisor has a way of making his people "look good." Workers in his sphere come to realize that their own ideas are valuable, possibly because of a little "twist" he puts on them or an extra fact he offers in their support. And they also see that their own feelings are worth stating frankly and directly with dignity. They are not under pressure to justify everything they do.

In the department next door, the exact opposite may be true. The supervisor has a knack for making people feel foolish. He has ways of making everyone dependent on him. I know of one military officer, for example, who so affected his junior officers that they would tighten up, feel stupid, and say things they did not mean to say. He was a bright officer with a good sense of humor, but his talents were not administrative in nature.

Employees have freedom to make mistakes. The person who guesses wrong or "goofs" does not lose managerial favor. Prides can be hurt, and tempers can flare, but his self-respect is not undermined because of a mistake. (That does not mean he is never fired—far from it. As long as he is on the staff, however, his inadequacies are accepted, and he is respected.) When the administrator does indulge in fault-finding, he usually concentrates on procedures rather than on people.

One company president calls the freedom to make mistakes the *first* freedom that management should support. He observes:

It seems to me that too many of our companies today overpenalize the mistake and undercredit the fresh and new. I can't think of anything which annoys me more than the man who says: here's the way we handled it last year—and the year before—and we'd better handle it the same way this year. . . .

Sometimes we forget how eager we were to try out our new ideas. All our people, I'm sure, have new ideas, too. They're itching to take a crack at putting them into practice, to swim in a little deeper water and justify their membership on the team. Good. You give them the chance. *But* maybe the idea doesn't work out quite so well. If there's a reprimand, what happens? Every time that enterprising spirit is broken down even a little, every time that little spark or originality is snuffed out, we are choking off the very taproots of our organization's precious fund of creativity.[1]

Operating methods and procedures tend to reflect the preferences of the employees on the job. There is strict emphasis on good results and performance, but people are not subject to directives governing every motion and act except in special circumstances—for instance, where safety, public relations, or a unique production problem is concerned. The administrator knows the

---

1. William T. Brady, "The Freedom to Make Mistakes," an address delivered in November, 1959 (obtainable from Corn Products Company, New York, N.Y.).

dangers of trying too hard to "engineer" behavior. He has seen what happens when that is done. The supervisor who insists that workers keep their desks tidy or who frowns at "unbusinesslike" procedures may be quite sincere in his attempt to increase efficiency. It so often happens, however, that when he controls these habits, productiveness goes down rather than up. In part, no doubt, this result is due to resentment. But it is perhaps also true that these habits and patterns of which he disapproves have a subtle "built-in" function that he fails to understand.

As an illustration, let us take the case of "American Radia-tronics Corporation" (the name is disguised). This case involves a certain production group, which, under a new general foreman, has developed one of the finest profit and quality records of any unit in the corporation, a leading producer in the nuclear electronics industry. The operators have been allowed to work out many of their own methods and systems, however, and the latter do not follow the "book" of the industrial engineer. The place has a kind of messiness and disorganization about it that upsets a technical specialist from the central staff. He tells the case-writer:

I really cannot understand how this operation makes money. The products are primitive in design, no changes have been made in years, and there's no engineering control of any kind. Everything is run on a casual hit or miss basis. It shouldn't make money, but somehow it does. . . .

Dollarwise they're doing a pretty good job in here, as far as it goes, but they've got one overriding weakness in the way they are presently set up. Do you realize the girls do all their own testing in here? The same girls that make the tubes test them. It just isn't logical. Human nature is that way. You can't trust the same people who make something to also test it. It's not healthy. They'll always try to protect themselves. This group of test equipment over here should be operated by a distinctly separate group of people completely removed from the production and under different supervision. That's the only basis under which you can get reliable testing and guard against infiltration of loyalties back and forth between manufacturing and testing. . . .

We've got plans in the works for taking on this place and really making it over. And when we do we'll see to it that the testing operations are carried on in a separate department. We'll really whip this operation into shape. . . .

There's a tremendous potential in this kind of activity, but it's never been exploited. We've got [all kinds of] designs on the board right now that would revolutionize the way of doing things here if we could get them going. I'd like to make this a model show place for the company. Right now it's the worst in the company. Look at all this dirt around and the disorganization. . . .

This place has never been under engineering control. . . . They design their own products, they alter and maintain their own production equipment and processes, and they are free to go off in all different directions at once. The first thing we would do if we could get hold of this room would be to put every operation under close engineering surveillance. The whole setup needs to be revamped and overhauled from one end to the other. We'll do it too. You won't recognize it two years from now. Some of the new products we have in mind will call for a level of sophistication in production methods, equipment design, and cleanliness that'll make this look sick. You've seen pictures of how some of these production departments look in other companies—cleanliness precautions that make them look like operating rooms, temperature and humidity controls, all white painted walls and equipment. That's what we'll have here.[2]

Possibly this efficiency engineer may be able to make the organization more productive than the foreman did, but clearly he will have a different effect on the operators. They will no longer be working out their own testing procedures and worker relationships. They will never let dust balls gather under the benches. They will not take the long route to another part of the room. They will not be working and acting in many ways that have been perfectly satisfactory to their foreman *so long as* they have turned out good work.

And who knows? Does the logical mind of the staff technician really understand all there is to understand about this picture?

---

2. American Radiatronics Corporation (A), a Harvard Business School case, pp. 37-38. Copyright 1960 by the President and Fellows of Harvard College.

Possibly, for instance, the informality that strikes him as "disorganization" serves a purpose. It may help to make the atmosphere more congenial to the operators, which in turn perhaps makes them more productive. Again, perhaps the messiness that the technician abhors contributes to their fine performance. It may be their way of showing their independence—visible evidence that they *are* running the job as the foreman has indicated he is willing to let them do. If that show of independence is taken away from them, as the efficiency man intends, perhaps they will demonstrate their power in another way—by a slow-down, for example, or by letting opportunities for improvement slip by.

Employees have a sense of mission and purpose. They are not simply doing as they are told. Nor are they working in particular ways simply because those are the ways they worked last year. They understand that their purpose and the purpose of their agency or division is not simply to survive. They have a mission. They are helping to meet important needs, and they are creating needs. In the process, they generate and regenerate a sense of common effort, of interrelationship and interdependence, of unity. Quarreling and conflict may be excited by this striving, but they do not stand in its way.

The sense of mission is quite likely to be accompanied by considerable interest in invention and innovation, in planning and control, and in quantitative data that cut across departmental lines. It may also show up in the form of cockiness and aggressiveness. "By the end of the 1930's . . . Humble employees, it is said, had begun to think of themselves as the 'prima donnas' of the oil industry." And they did not hesitate to bargain hard and ably for their interests in negotiations with management.[3] Perhaps the most telling evidence of the sense of mission is a strong interest in "action" or "what-to-do" questions. In particular, managers and

---

3. Henrietta M. Larson and Kenneth Wiggins Porter, *History of Humble Oil & Refining Company* (New York: Harper & Brothers, 1959), pp. 387-388.

employees want to please people *outside* the organization. This preoccupation has a way of creeping in and coloring the whole atmosphere of the organization's work. O. A. Ohmann of Standard Oil Company of Ohio once made these notes about an "extremely successful executive" he knew:

> In his general behavior he moves without haste or hysteria. He is typically well organized, relaxed, and confident, even under trying circumstances. There is a high degree of consistency in his behavior and in the quality of his decisions because his basic values do not shift. Since he does not operate by expediency, others can depend on him; and this consistency makes for efficiency in the discharge of delegated responsibility. Those operating problems which do come to him for decision seem to move easily and quickly to a conclusion. . . . In policy-level discussions his contributions have a natural quality of objectivity because "self-concern" does not confuse. Others take him at face value because his motives are not suspect. When differences or conflicts do arise, his approach is not that of compromise; rather he attempts to integrate the partisan views around mutually acceptable longer-range goals. The issues of the moment then seem to dissolve in a discussion of the best means to the achievement of the objective.[4]

Here is an episode from the Nunn-Bush Shoe Company during the depression of 1921:

> The workers knew of the personal economy measures taken by the officers. They knew we had sold our automobiles and used streetcars for transportation. They knew of many other sacrifices that officers were making in their attempt to relieve the situation. Several bench-worker stockholders came to me and expressed their willingness to purchase more stock in the company, if that would help. The business agent of the Association suggested that, if I felt it necessary, a good part of the combined resources of the workers might be made available. During the entire period our workers did not raise a single problem that would add more troubles to those we already had.[5]

---

4. " 'Skyhooks,' With Special Implications for Monday Through Friday," *Harvard Business Review*, May-June, 1955, p. 40.

5. Henry L. Nunn, *The Whole Man Goes to Work* (New York: Harper & Brothers, 1953), p. 81.

There is a feeling of responsibility for the results of decisions. As a matter of fact, supervisors down the line may imagine themselves more accountable for results than they really are. As an illustration, let us take the case of a deck-division officer on a Navy cargo ship. If we look at the decisions this officer makes, it is clear that he alone does not answer for what happens. His decisions are carried out by petty officers who have received their training on other ships under other commands. The willingness of the winch operators and cargo handlers is heavily influenced by the general atmosphere of the ship, for which he alone is not responsible. At any one moment, furthermore, a seaman may be thinking of many past experiences that have made him bitter or resentful, willing or co-operative and that have induced him to react, not only to the job he is doing, but to memories superimposed on top of that job as well.

Accordingly, when our division officer gives his orders of the day, all sorts of things can go wrong that are beyond his personal power to control. If the winches are operated carelessly or the cargo loaded in the wrong way, he is probably justified most of the time in putting at least part of the blame on somebody else. "The morale on this ship is terrible, and it's the Commander's fault. . . . " Or, "The kids we get from shore these days don't want to work. In World War II we would've done this job with half as many men and they would've done it a damn sight better . . . "

This kind of attitude is common, and almost always someone is urging it on management, yet it need not dominate our division officer's thinking. His approach can be instead to assume personal responsibility for the quality of effort under his command, regardless of the obstacles. If the men are not responsive to his and his petty officers' directions, he can seek tirelessly to *make* them so—knowing that response can never be perfect, yet teaching the standards and conditions of perfection. If the winch operators do a lot of day-dreaming, he can work to *develop* high standards of alertness and accuracy, higher than he will probably ever get but not too high to strive for. He can endeavor to stir up the will to succeed, the feeling of mastery over the spirit.

The history of organizations is in fact sprinkled liberally with examples of this approach. The following illustration, provided by the general foreman of a large mill, involves the work of a foreman down the line who has charge of a certain shift:

> One Sunday morning on the twelve to eight shift, the crane broke down. My shift foreman called the mechanical department, and asked them to repair the crane immediately. The mechanical people said they could not do the job, that they would have to call in the millwrights, pipe-fitters, and so on. They said, "We cannot do that without the approval of our superintendent." He said, "You call those men right away because this crane is stopping the production, and I can't afford to lose that production." There was some reluctance from the mechanical people to do that, but my foreman insisted that he was taking on himself the whole repsonsibility of this decision. Finally, the mechanical people decided to call the repair crew and the whole thing was repaired before eight in the morning.[6]

Subordinates try to work out as many problems as they can through each other rather than through formal chains of authority. Organizational people do not relate themselves only to the man in charge. A diagram of the relationships of a group and its boss would show a pattern less like the spokes of a wheel emanating from a hub than like a cobweb in which the braces and stays between the radial threads are at least as important as the radial threads themselves:

> "I usually can get things done with Frank Goodwin in the finishing department," continued Blanchard [assistant production manager in a paper mill]. "He trained me right. Over a long period of time he taught me to be careful in the way I deal with him. . . . If for any reason he is away, of course I don't hesitate to talk to Hank Crawford in the plain paper section of the finishing department, or to Allen on a coated specialty paper. I'm always careful, however, to ask them to talk to Frank about the problem when he gets back.

---

6. William Foote Whyte, *Men At Work* (Homewood, Illinois: Dorsey Press and Richard D. Irwin, Inc., 1961), p. 441.

"When I go down through the mill, naturally I see things that ought to be changed or the men tell me about things that need improvements. I generally talk to Crawford or even to Phillips or McColl [supervisors in the finishing department] about things there, and in one way or another they seem to get done. I don't know exactly what happens. I suppose they go to Frank and say something like, 'I was talking to Paul Blanchard the other day and such and such seemed like a good idea. What do you think?' Discussing a problem and leaving the conclusion for them to act upon seems to work pretty well with the men who are about my own age."

[Blanchard then proceeds to tell the case writer about a man named Prout with whom he has had much difficulty. Prout has just refused to talk over the telephone with Blanchard about a production problem, and the case writer asks the assistant what he is going to do. "Well, I guess I had better go down and talk it over with Mr. Prout," Blanchard replies. "We will have to work out something."][7]

It is significant that the assistant production manager works things out with *other* assistants and their bosses. He does not send every operating problem up to his boss to decide, then do the leg-work for him in carrying it out.

The administrator does not get this effect easily. We know from many clinical studies how important the informal group is in the life of a factory or office, yet a capable manager may have a hard time getting his assistants to work out their problems informally among themselves. For instance, when James Richard was in charge of a manufacturing operation employing several hundred men, supervisors often tried to get him to intervene in their problems with one another. He generally refused because he felt it would weaken their interrelationships. He wrote that one day he was visited by a foreman troubled by his workers' complaints that they could not get overtime pay, while the men in another department, headed by foreman X, could get it. The first foreman criticized X's practices: "He has got a bunch of women there, and one good man could do what three of those women do

---

in a day, and that is the reason why he has got to bring those
guys in on Saturday to get caught up on his work." Wouldn't
James Richard do something about it? After all, it was important
to keep production costs down. Richard wrote:

> He could not face the other foremen directly; he insisted it was
> my job to do that. I told him that I realized his problem with his
> own men was acute, that I could convey his problem to the other
> foremen but not his judgments about the women workers in the
> other department. I also said that I was reluctant to carry this com-
> munication and hoped we might someday reach a point where each
> man felt free to carry his feelings directly to the others involved.
> I really did not know whether his judgments were justified, and I
> said so. However, I indicated a willingness to sit in with both of
> them to discuss it. The foreman declined this offer.[8]

At first the foremen resisted his approach. They would argue
that his intervention was needed because "I think it's your job"
or "You're calling the shots." It took him some time to convince
them that a strong enterprise was *not* one in which he arbitrated
all the disputes and differences.

*There is an air of confidence that the organization can deal
with any problem that arises.* There is more willingness to look
into the teeth of difficulties that threaten the enterprise from outside. Because whatever the trouble may be, employees feel that
they can meet it—not eliminate it, necessarily, but live with it
successfully.

In a well-managed business, executives are not likely to shun
market research because they are afraid of it or to try under-
cutting the union because they fear its popularity among workers.
In a well-managed military unit minority views are less likely to
be suppressed from fear they will upset existing policies. In a
well-managed hospital, there is less likely to be embarrassment
over "politics" in the administration. People are willing to "open
up" discussion rather than to control it or constrict it.

---

8. James Richard, "Group-Centered Leadership in an Industrial Organization: A Case Study," in Thomas Gordon, ed., *Group-Centered Leadership*
(Boston: Houghton Mifflin Company, 1955), p. 328.

The organization is not bent on security. It is not preoccupied with efforts to fix its markets or control Capitol Hill. It is determined to develop the ability to handle any problem that arises. More men than usual are likely to exhibit versatility and flexibility in thinking about their jobs and futures. "I've been just about everything in this company," a senior executive in a New England firm told me once. "I was in accounting long ago, and in the recession I was the sales manager. Once I had quite a bit to do with research, even. Now it's public relations. Ten years from now, who knows? Why, we may be in a different business, for all I can tell. But I'll be trying to stay with it, whatever happens."

The everyday conflicts, misunderstandings, and unpleasantries of organizational life gain meaning and significance. The strong organization offers many satisfactions, but it is also a source of unpleasantness. Tempers fly, and there are misunderstandings; mistakes are made, and injustices are done; sacrifices are made in a strenuous common effort, and the effort fails.

The task of the managerial mind is not to eliminate this suffering but to give meaning to it. Employees become more interested in the mutual values to be *gained* from facing up to an issue or breaking up an old pattern. Certainly this attitude is of no little significance, and to appreciate it we need only to contrast it with the approach of the legal mind. In the courtroom, the emphasis is on justice. Plaintiff and defendant argue their sides of the case, and the judge or jury generally makes an award to one at the expense of the other. This process is called "adjudication."

In the administrative process, too, a kind of adjudication may enter in at one stage or another but only as one step along the way rather than the end itself. The managerial emphasis is on the creative, on the effort to "save" something from the struggle so that the participants can reunite and move forward again.

To illustrate this effect and its relationship to administrative action, let us take two common examples, both in industrial relations, where the possibility of continued degeneration is always present. The first case involves a cloth inspector named Irene Mason, who was discharged from a small woolen-textile factory. She was fired for talking back to the foreman, interfering with his work, and in other ways making a pest of herself. A man named DuFresne, the business agent of the union, demanded that Irene Mason be given her job back. In arguing the case with the superintendent, Smolokas, and the assistant mill manager, Forbes, the union agent stuck stubbornly to his original demand, despite counter-offers and pressure from the company men:

DUFRESNE: I'm not interested in another job for her. I want her back in her old job. She came to the union with her grievance, and we're going to do something for her, even if we have to go to arbitration. I told her I thought she had a good case and would go to bat for her, and I'm not going to let her down. What d'you think would happen to the union if I didn't do something about cases like this?

FORBES: Well, Mr. DuFresne, just what will happen here if we put her back, supposing we do? Will that help anything? There is a clash of personalities here that just can't be remedied. We've tried enough times, but it won't work. She'll do the same thing again.

DUFRESNE: What I want you to do is to give us a chance to show how the union can help you. If you put the girl back, I'll call her in and have a good talk with her. I'll tell her that, even though this is a free country, she shouldn't express opinions that don't involve her, especially if they are insulting to management. I'll tell her that she is expected to do her work.

SMOLOKAS: Well, what if she does the same things all over again, as she will? If it is wrong for her to do them then, why wasn't it just as wrong for her to do them last Saturday and before? I don't understand the difference.

DUFRESNE: The difference is this. You have given the union the chance to see what it can do to straighten this girl out. Then if she doesn't come around, we won't go to bat for her again. I'll tell her it will be her last chance.

FORBES: But why should you do that? Isn't that management's job? Do we have to depend on the union to discipline our workers?

DUFRESNE: You can do whatever you like. But we want a chance to show you that we can be helpful, too. . . . [9]

The second incident concerns a manufacturing plant. A mechanic named Renault had been laid off by one of the foremen. When the union investigated, it learned that another mechanic named Parkman was taking over the job. The union president then demanded that Renault be reinstated because he had higher seniority than Parkman. Management resisted the demand but finally had to back down because it had no sound rating system or performance data to justify its decision. Some of the dialogue recorded in the argument is revealing, however. It took place in the office of the supervisor of industrial relations, Avery; the foreman, Carter, was present along with Renault and the union president, Cameron:

RENAULT: I claim that I can do all the work that is required.

CARTER: No one disputes your claim. You can do the work all right, but you can't do it as well as Parkman. And I can't be expected to run my department efficiently if I can't select the best men to do the job.

CAMERON: Well, this doesn't get us anywhere. If we can't settle the case here, we're prepared to take it to top management.

AVERY: If you mean by that remark that a settlement not in your favor isn't a settlement, you'd better take it to top management right now. My job is to see that all the cards are on the table and that every man is treated fairly. After all, it's up to Mr. Carter to decide whether or not he wants to keep this man.

CAMERON: All we're interested in is the fact that Renault has 11 years' service and that he can do the work.

AVERY: True enough, but Renault's been with Carter only 2 years, and we all know that the work he did before was not at all similar to ours. I can only agree with Mr. Carter that a foreman's job is to run his department efficiently, in a slack period as well as in a boom. Naturally, when his work is dropping down, he's going to keep the ablest fellow.

---

9. Paul Pigors and Charles A. Myers, *Personnel Administration* (New York: McGraw-Hill Book Company, Inc., 1956), p. 528.

CARTER: Well, I'll tell you what we'll do, gentlemen. I'd be willing to take Renault back if he will buckle down to business, not kick every time he's assigned some work, and just begin to realize that his ability means something to him from the standpoint of keeping his job as well as seniority. I don't want to get involved in a squabble, but Mr. Renault's got to learn that 11 years of service with the company and membership in a union do not guarantee him the opportunity to stall on the job.

AVERY: Well, how is that with you fellows?

CAMERON: That's O.K. with me.

RENAULT: Me, too.

AVERY: I'm willing to go along with this, too, provided Mr. Renault fully understands what was said. *(To Renault:)* And, Mr. Renault, that doesn't mean the foreman is going to watch you like a hawk in an endeavor to find an excuse to fire you. Neither do we expect you to go back to the department with an "I told you so" attitude. That's not going to help the situation at all. All it means is that now you have an opportunity to prove to these gentlemen what you can do.[10]

In both of these incidents the issues are petty and irritating by some standards. But let us look further. In the Irene Mason case, the union agent is not content simply to have the argument settled. He wants to "save" something from it, to build on it. He wants to use the incident to symbolize the union's willingness to help with discipline and productivity. He wants the episode to dignify the role of the union and, through it, the workers. Accordingly, while management is forced to make concessions, it does not really lose—or at least the union manager does not intend it to lose. His action reflects union policies that, in this respect at least, exhibit a strong commitment to the human organization.

In the case of Pierre Renault, both the foreman and the industrial relations executive back down. They could say, in effect, "Okay, smart guys, you win this time—but wait and see, we'll get even." But they do not. They take a more constructive attitude: "We'll put Renault back on the job, but let's give some

---

10.   *Ibid.*, pp. 498-499.

meaning to this squabble. Both workers and managers have a stake in good work, for all the troubles they get into with each other, and let's see that this decision becomes a step in the right direction." They thus dignify the role of everyone in the case. It is not simply a matter of saving face. They are showing their determination that employees shall become not victims of friction but masters of it, capable of making it serve *their* ends. Their efforts reflect the thinking of the larger management group of which they are a part.

There is less anxiety about conflict and its implications. Managers and workers become interested in removing, not conflict, but the *anxieties* of conflict. They accept the necessity of struggle itself—but not of dire consequences on their feelings toward each other.

Again, the everyday illustrations are the most helpful. For instance, in another case reported by Pigors and Myers, the workers in a manufacturing plant complained to management that an acid dipper was receiving a finish polisher's pay, which was higher.[11] They were especially irritated because the acid dipper was boasting about his status. The union representative took up the case, and, after the usual charges and countercharges had been aired and some sharp remarks had been passed, it turned out that the workman in question was not being paid on the higher scale at all.

If the aim of the session had been adjudication, both management and the union would have been content to stop there and go back to work. But the foreman of the department, named O'Rourke, wanted to remove any suspicion that he considered workers' complaints a bother. "I didn't know that Wilson [the workman] was doing any bragging," he told the union representative. "I do wish that you fellows would come to me first instead of bringing me on the carpet with Mr. Avery [the industrial relations director]." Avery took up the same theme. "Before

---

11. *Ibid.,* p. 542.

we adjourn," he said, "I should like to add for the information of all of you that you should feel free at any time to see me if anything is bothering you. On the other hand, we expect that you have and will continue to have confidence in your foreman and will discuss matters with him first."

Neither he nor O'Rourke felt concern—or thought they should feel concern—over the *presence* of conflict. In effect, they said, "Misunderstandings are natural, and let's not apologize for them or try to suppress them. Let's try to bring them out into the open more often." They wanted to open up the channels of talk—in order to relieve needless worries over the possibility of blame. Smith, the union representative, said, "Well, if he shows a willingness to talk with us, I'm sure we'll be glad to talk with him." Avery then asked O'Rourke for a similar commitment, and he gladly gave it.

Efforts to remove anxieties over conflict have, it seems to me, an extraordinary effect on the resiliency of employee relations. The following incident, involving a capable group leader named Dottie and an errant operator on a conveyor line, is drawn from a careful study of foremen relations (the "rough" talk was characteristic in the plant):

Dottie openly "bawled out" operator #1 when he inserted a part incorrectly which delayed another operator further along the line. When Dottie learned of the faulty installation she yelled out, "Operator #1! Come over here, you bad kid." Operator #1 came over and said, "What can I do for you?" Dottie shouted, "What can you do? Look at this! You jerk! If this happens again I'll slap you so hard you'll be spitting blood for a week. Now don't ever let me see this again, G-- D--- it, or I'll let you have it." While Dottie was bawling out operator #1, she had a half smile on her face. The other operators in her section were watching the incident and were laughing. Even operator #1 seemed to be enjoying the incident somewhat since he had a sheepish grin on his face. He left Dottie without appearing the least bit upset or sulky.[12]

---

12. A. Zaleznik, *Foreman Training in a Growing Enterprise* (Boston: Division of Research, Harvard Business School, 1951), p. 104.

In this case, the supervisor must have succeeded so well in removing fears over failure that not even a rough bawling out could be taken as a personal threat. The operator knew that no one was waiting to fire him, that, no matter what he did, he would always be given a chance to do better if he kept on trying. These convictions gave him the ability to "bounce back" as he might never have been able to do in a more judicial atmosphere.

THE ELUSIVE ELEMENT

If these effects of the managerial mind on employees are viewed all together, one curious and remarkable feature stands out: The manager cannot by himself produce them. He can ask for them, hope for them, and play a strong supporting role, but only the *other* people in the organization actually have the power to produce them. While admirers and press agents may dramatize the wonderful power of a leader, the organization has a more awesome power still.

Naturally, an executive with jobs, promotions, and salaries at his command can get subordinates to do what he tells them to do, if his requests are clear and reasonable. He can, in effect, create a tremendous computer of flesh and blood that will carry out the instructions he gives it. But if his organization is competing with other organizations—whether in education, war, government, or business—it is not enough that his people follow his orders. They must put their own wills and intelligence into the project, or success will belong to the rivals who do. Whatever the quality that makes employees want to strive through endless conflicts and misunderstandings toward a common goal, the manager does not create it. His "chance to be an especially good or especially bad man," to use Robert Hutchins' phrase, lies more in his capacity to create *opportunities* for response than in his ability to direct what that response shall be.

IMPLICATIONS FOR INDIVIDUALS

What are some of the implications of these yardsticks for managers and would-be managers?

1. *You have got to be willing to be judged by imprecise standards.* Don't consider administration as a career if you are the kind of person who needs precise gauges of success. You won't have a won-and-lost record like a baseball pitcher or a trial lawyer; you can't judge your success by the amount you are worth, like a trader or "wheeler and dealer." Nevertheless, your work is subject to standards, and despite their lack of precision they are demanding standards, hard to meet, and of the utmost importance to society.

2. *To improve your managerial ability, you must be willing to work for people under you as well as for people over you.* The kind of person who is interested only in pleasing the boss can scarcely hope to measure up well by the yardsticks described.

3. *You should be a person who does not mind having other people around you receiving credit.* Some of your best work will be done in relative anonymity, with subordinates and associates receiving more credit than you do.

4. *You will be happier if you are not a perfectionist.* Not only is perfection practically impossible by any one of the nine yardsticks, but in some ways great success by one measure will reduce success by another. (For example, the stronger one group's feeling of mission, the more cocky and single-minded it might become, hence the poorer its sense of relationship might be with other groups in the organization.) What is more, sometimes the realities of political life—getting ahead, job security, etc.—militate against building up others' confidence and power, although I think this conflict is greatly exaggerated in fiction and popular reading.

5. *You need a faith in the workings of things you do not wholly understand.* You cannot always "see" certain results flowing from your leadership, as an engineer can see results in a machine or an accountant can see conclusions developing from a mass of raw data. You must be willing to work your way and "let things happen" in their own good time.

11

IS

THE

MANAGERIAL

MIND

CREATIVE?

DOES THE ADMINISTRATOR *create* anything? Does the managerial mind help him to make a contribution in the sense that a scientist or teacher contributes—to leave the world with new structures, tools, and approaches? Or is emphasis on innovation lost in his preoccupation with turning out goods and services? When great steps forward are made in business, government, and education, are they made by entrepreneurs, statesmen, and intellectual leaders rather than by managers?

Such questions underlie much criticism and disparagement of the administrative function—from university scholars who scoff at degrees in business administration to satirists of the "organization man." While these questions lead us to look again at certain problems previously examined in this volume, the perspective is so different and the topic so important that separate consideration is justified.

My conclusion is that both defenders *and* critics of managerial creativity are right—up to a point. After that point, some of the very things that lead critics to minimize the administrator's contribution actually help him to produce, to innovate, to create.

VOICES OF DISPARAGEMENT

What are the bases for minimizing the manager's contribution?

Parasitic role. One of the more common criticisms—usually not stated so bluntly as I shall put it here—is that the administrator's role is secondary in importance. He helps to keep things moving, of course, but his main function is to adjust, to control, to persuade, and so forth. He is not a prime contributor, the critics argue. He does not create.

One of the nicest expressions of this complaint is in John Marquand's novel, *Sincerely, Willis Wayde.* Willis is a young man at Harcourt Mill who finds favor with the owners and begins his climb in management. One day after five o'clock, he and his father drive home together. The father wears a blue work shirt and baggy trousers; his old Model T, though battered on the outside, has an engine that works like clockwork. Willis, by contrast, already has the well-groomed "managerial look." The following conversation occurs at one point in their drive:

"Listen, boy," he said. "People are divided into two parts—people who do things and the rest, who live off those who do things. Now I may not amount to much, but I've had a pretty happy time, because I can turn out something. I can do anything in that damn mill that anyone else can do, and they all know it, boy. Well, maybe you'll spend your life living off other people's doings, but if you have to, don't fool yourself. Maybe you'll end up like Harcourt. I don't know. But you'll never *be* like Harcourt."

There was a good deal in what his father had said, and Willis realized it even then. He was listening to the age-old definition of management and labor. . . .

"But you like Mr. Harcourt, don't you?" Willis asked.

"Hell, yes," Alfred Wayde said. "All his moving parts are greased. He knows what he is, and we get along, but he lives off me just the same."

"Well, you live off him, too, don't you?" Willis said.

"All right," Alfred Wayde answered, "all right. There always has to be a boss in the front office. I only say, don't try too hard, Willis, or else you'll end up a son of a bitch." [1]

Those who share this point of view can cite any number of incidents to support their case. They refer to companies where the layers of management have been shuffled and reshuffled without greatly affecting the fortunes of the organizations because, it is claimed, the real backbones of such firms are the researchers, the engineers, or the salesmen. They point to organizations where management functions like industrial relations or planning have been cut in size or eliminated without untoward results. They remember small firms that have risen on the sheer strength of their owner-managers' inventive genius. They mention names like Thomas Edison or Henry Ford, who "weren't mere administrators, *they created things.*"

A recent variation of this theme appears in discussions of the needs of underdeveloped countries. For instance, Sir Charles Snow has argued that the "have" countries of the West should make an all-out effort to staff the "have-not" nations with scientists, engineers, and technicians. Sir Charles believes that their talents can help the other nations to industrialize, to bridge the technological gap in a few years. Managers are conspicuous by their absence. Clearly, the administrative contribution is not regarded as a creative one.

---

1. John Marquand, *Sincerely, Willis Wayde* (Boston: Little, Brown and Company, 1955), pp. 99-100.

Lack of entrepreneurial vision. Another common complaint is that the managerial mind is so preoccupied with operating detail that he applies little imagination to the purposes organization could serve. Afflicted with this organizational myopia, the manager fails to see new social and economic needs. It is alleged that he loses any instinct to pioneer, to "think big."

This complaint usually comes from those who idealize the entrepreneur. To them, the exciting thing is the building of organizations. They would find the attitudes described in Chapters 1 and 5 dull and uninspired. "This is not real leadership," they would say. "It is not of such stuff that the men who make history are made." They are likely to idealize instead the leadership of such men as Woodrow Wilson, who instigated the Federal Reserve Act, Federal Trade Commission Act, and other legislation; of Ezra Cornell, who founded a great new university; of Edward Ball, who pioneered in the development of Florida real estate; of Clinton Murchison, who founded a natural-gas empire.

Businessmen who share this point of view dislike the word, "administrator." One business leader told me, "I don't call our top people 'administrators.' I call them *'executives.'* When I think of administrators, I think of bureaucrats."

Lack of depth. Another common reason for criticizing the administrative mind is the allegation that it tends to be shallow or imprecise. It is said, for instance, that a professional administrator devotes so much time to operations that he does not have much time to think. There is no "culture" of administration, no body of knowledge accumulated over the years and passed on in professional training. In law, there are volumes rich in principles and rules and exceptions developed over hundreds of years. In science, there is the precision of measurement and controlled experiment. In education, there is a storehouse of wisdom and insight filled by the world's greatest minds.

What comparable tradition, it is asked, has administration? Do not the administrator's assumptions—like those described in Chapter 7—indicate clearly that he is merely feeling his way?

This prejudice is reflected in the attitudes of professional people and of experts, consultants, and staff specialists who are themselves on organizational payrolls. They respect the administrator for his hard work and skill, but they would not trade places with him. "He is not a thinker," they say, "and ideas rule the world."

Conformity. Then there is the complaint that the managerial mind encourages conformity. Critics in this school may agree with the arguments in Chapter 3 about the importance of differences, but in practice, they argue, administrative values tend to produce an "organization man" who "plays the game" and resists originality and risk-taking.

Their favorite evidence is the styling of American automobiles. The new-product manager in Detroit, they argue, is not going to risk a salary running into many thousands of dollars by innovating. He is far more certain of success if he goes along with the crowd (including competitors)—efficient industrial intelligence tells him a year in advance about the main changes other car manufacturers are going to make, and it is easy for him to follow.

THE NATURE OF ADMINISTRATIVE CREATIVITY

Surely we cannot lightly dismiss such criticisms. We cannot insist that they are all wrong. Organizations *have* grown from the efforts of technical and sales people without benefit of administrators; Florida realty and Texas natural gas would not have boomed the way they did without Ed Ball, Clint Murchison, and other entrepreneurs; administrators cannot make precise contributions to the rich tradition of professional knowledge, as the lawyer or scientist can; there *is* a rein on idea men in well-managed organizations.

Previous chapters—on the value placed on differences, problem hunting, high expectations, or teaching—do not deny these facts.

It is important to see, however, that it is partly *because* these things are true that the administrator *can* make an original and creative contribution to the world. More specifically:

1. In order to put and keep one creative idea in operation, the administrator must "put the brakes" on many other good ideas.

2. When the administrator examines a concept originated by an entrepreneur or other leader, he is likely to give it new form and shape through his own decisions and actions translating it into practice.

3. The spirit, flexibility, and maneuverability that a good administrator breathes into an organization are themselves a contribution of a high creative order.

These points are worth considering in more detail.

Selective innovation. While some administrators may turn down twenty new ideas for every one they accept and while they may be adept at refusing to reopen questions and entertain improvements, it is still true that managers make countless innovations of all types. I think it was Dennis Robinson, President of High Voltage Engineering Corporation and himself a scientist and entrepreneur, who once commented that important new inventions in his industry are usually the product of both a technical man *and* an important executive. Among innovations with which we are all familiar—new drugs, new kinds of hospital, new developments in commercial transportation, new ways of disseminating knowledge, advances in space, breakthroughs in military technology—who can deny that, in case after case, the key men were what we call "management-oriented."

The administrator does not, however, merely conceive an idea or help in its conception; he also follows it through many stages. He sells it. His mission is to make it a reality, and for this purpose he organizes and administers. Once he commits himself in this way, he must necessarily rule out many possibilities for further innovation. When a decision is made to operate in a particular manner, he *must* become adept at turning away the man who proposes a new idea, a further improvement, or a previously overlooked fact. When employees have already been launched on a certain combination of jobs and procedures to follow, he *must* rule out most second thoughts. If he does not, nothing will be accomplished—for in an alert, thinking, creative group of people there will be no end of ideas for improvement.

The illusion of conformity is thus created, even in the most extreme cases of management commitment to invention and innovation.

Small companies offer the easiest illustration, although what is true of them in this respect is true of innumerable divisions and departments of larger organizations. For example, there is a small firm in Puerto Rico that makes a special kind of sun screen. For a number of years, this firm has been basically a one-product, one-idea company. This does not mean, however, that the owner-manager (and co-inventor of the original product) has not entertained seriously a great many other inventions and innovations. He has. But to bring one new product through many stages of trial, development, partial failure, redevelopment, and success—hampered by war, strikes, shortages, production difficulties, and so forth—he has had to avoid exploring far in new directions. The intensity of creative effort he has put into following the basic invention through has been at least as great, in my opinion, as that he would have had to apply to the initial development stages of other inventions he has considered.

For a second illustration, let me offer quite a different situation. I would guess that even those in the "literary set" (from which spring some of the sharpest deprecations of the administrative point of view) would agree that *The New Yorker* was one of the most important innovations in magazine publishing in the first half of the twentieth century. It was, and is, a fresh, original, and sophisticated departure from the big slicks and pulps. Now James Thurber has written an intimate account of *The Years With Ross*. Thurber had, I am sure, no intention of making an administrative case study, yet there are a number of places in the book where Harold Ross the administrator shines through as clearly as Harold Ross the eccentric, individualist, creator, and humorist. For instance, it is made clear that quite a few "idea men" must have become disillusioned with Ross's refusal to branch into material on social issues:

> Harold Ross, inherently cautious, fundamentally conservative, stuck resolutely to his original belief that the *New Yorker* was not a magazine designed to step tides, join crusades, or take political stands. He was not going to print a lot of "social-conscious stuff," because his intuition told him that, if he did, he would be overwhelmed by it. He has been accused of timidity—and he had a lot of that—of evasion of responsibility, and of the loss of his chance to turn his magazine into a voice of protest and rebellion. The *New Yorker*, he staunchly contended, was not the *New Republic* or the *Nation;* it wanted superior prose, funny drawings, and sound journalism, without propaganda. He didn't encourage, he even discouraged, pieces on McCarthyism, and in a letter to Frank Sullivan, who had suggested writing a piece about his cliche expert and McCarthyism, he wrote, "I don't think so. I'd think twice about it. I can't see it myself, and if I can't see a thing, I'm usually right." [2]

This example is useful because the ideas Ross turned down were good ones (*The New Yorker* could probably have made a superb contribution to social understanding); one cannot say they were unintelligent proposals from people who did not understand good journalism. Nor can it be argued that during this period Ross had lost the innovative streak he had demonstrated in earlier years, for he did support some important changes. Consequently, we have a clear case of a man who discouraged innovations (plural) *for the sake of innovation* (singular).

---

2. James Thurber, *The Years With Ross* (Boston: Atlantic Little, Brown and Company, 1959), p. 172.

It is possible, of course, to attribute this insistence on what might be called selective innovation to personality characteristics. The fact remains, however, that again and again the attitude is found in the thinking of managers. It is an important part, it seems to me, of the managerial mind.

Creative transformation. There is a second, quite different way in which the administrator innovates. Let me introduce it by going back to our earlier example of Texas' famed Clinton Murchison. I was once discussing the career of this famous entrepreneur with a young man who had just read a profile of him in *Fortune* (later reprinted in a book). The profile included such observations as the following:

> The deal's the thing for Murchison, and when he finds that his deal will "walk," he lets others get the ulcers setting it on its feet. Out of one deal spins another, and still another, and there can never be enough spinning. . . .
>
> Texans fail to understand how one man can watch over [his industrial empire]. . . . The essence of the answer is in the sort of remark that is apt to be made at the mention of Murchison's name. "Clint just dreams things up. Then he sits back and lets other people sweat doing the dirty work." That is said half-humorously, but it carries truth.[3]

This kind of business pioneering, the young man told me, was far more interesting to him than administration. He had studied business administration and knew how important it was, but "administering things" somehow did not strike him as very challenging.

Now, it does not detract from the tremendous contribution of entrepreneurs to point out that, in almost every case, the idea that the public comes to know—the idea that is transformed into operating reality—has taken on important new shape and substance as a result of the work of administrators. It is true that the original inspirational spark came from an enterpreneur, but it is

---

3. The Editors of Fortune, *The Art of Success* (New York: J. B. Lippincott Company, 1956), pp. 123, 137.

also important to recognize that the final form—the form that works and has value for society—includes additions like a rolled snowball. These additions are also the product of creative work. Where did they come from? From the men who "administered things," in my friend's words. In fact, I know that entrepreneurs like Murchison will be the first to tell you that many vital structures and products of the organizations associated with their names were created by operating executives who came in after the original financing and establishment. Sometimes the latter acted so independently that their work was not even known to the founder until after its completion.

Why is it so easy to forget this fact? The administrator's contribution tends to be relatively anonymous. It comes at the second and third stages, while the first stage, like the first stage of the space rocket we see launched on television, is the one that impresses itself on the public mind. We associate the Federal Reserve System with Woodrow Wilson's name, forgetting that a large part of this great organizational innovation was the work of federal and business executives who came in after Wilson. We think of Ford Motor Company as being Henry Ford's baby, although crucial parts of the organization were pioneered—not merely operated under a mandate but "dreamed up"—by men in the administrative set. We remember many famous landing craft of World War II as "Higgins boats," named after Andrew Jackson Higgins, the extraordinary builder who sold the original idea to the Navy Department, but we forget how much of the final product was inspired by "bureaucrats" in Washington and managers in the New York Shipbuilding Corporation, General Motors, various shipyards, and other organizations.

In short, publicity and "visibility" to the public do not seem to be among the rewards for good administration. A comment by the former President of E. I. du Pont de Nemours is pertinent here: "The more effective an executive, the more his own identity and personality blend into the background of his organization. Here is a queer paradox. The more able the man, the less he stands out, the greater his relative anonymity outside his own immediate circle." [4]

Perhaps more important still for its bearing on administrative thinking, the kind of contribution the manager makes is additional evidence of the value he places on being in the driver's seat, in control—on seeing that things get done. It does not satisfy him to be an "idea man." He wants to be an "idea-into-action" man. The difference is somewhat similar to that between the researcher and the teacher, the first emphasizing the discovery of knowledge and perhaps the formulation of new hypotheses, the other emphasizing conversion of these ideas into the thinking and values of students.

Living instrumentality. Finally, is not administration a highly creative act even in its most everyday sense? This point has been touched on in earlier chapters, but it can stand further emphasis. An organization, being a kind of life, *is* creativity. It is the opposite of anarchy and chaos, as the organization of a plant or animal body is the opposite of formless, undisciplined energy. What is more, there is always a potential for innovation in an organization. Managers are more and more inclined to think of their organizations as unique fusions of skills and abilities that can serve as vehicles for unending series of services. An educational organization for liberal arts students in peacetime converts to the teaching of supply and ordnance in wartime. A philanthropic organization dedicated to the cure of one disease turns to research on another when the first is eliminated. An air force organization first identified with propeller-driven planes becomes identified next with jets, then with missiles—the last a radically different problem from the first, yet handled by many of the same teams of officers.

To be sure, the nonmanagerial employees in these organizations also change. It is not the act of conversion itself that we

4. Crawford H. Greenewalt, *The Uncommon Man* (New York: McGraw-Hill Book Company, Inc., 1959), p. 66.

are emphasizing here. It is the value in the administrator's mind of having an instrument that can create not one but a succession of things. Remember that many of the values and attitudes described in previous chapters would not be so important if the organization were conceived as having one purpose. The attitudes toward differences, tension, problem-probing, expectations, manipulation, teaching, knowledge—all presume the desirability of being able to change, expand, revise, redirect. In other words, the administrator emphasizes the things he does because of the importance to him of innovation.

Take A. O. Smith Corporation, one of countless possible examples. The entrepreneur who founded it was C. J. Smith, an immigrant from England who opened a machine shop in Milwaukee in 1874 and was soon busily producing bicycles. Now, if the critical stereotypes of managerial activity outlined earlier in this chapter had prevailed, the managers of this shop would have been content to go on turning out bicycles, keeping production flowing, ironing out operator problems, and talking with visitors, customers, journalists, and so forth. But that is not what happened. When the automotive era came, the managers of this company converted part of their organization (by then greatly expanded) to the manufacture of car frames. In World War I, they committed part of their organization to the manufacture of aerial bombs. Next they used it to produce oil pipe, oil vessels, and brewing equipment, while retaining the automotive lines. In World War II, they turned part of their organization to the manufacture of casings for "block-buster" bombs.[5]

These changes—prompted generally, not by entrepreneurs, staff experts, "idea men" from consulting firms, or technical people, but by succeeding generations of managers—surely indicate a great interest in change and innovation. This interest had a chain effect, enlarging the horizons of creativity for a superb engineering staff and providing valuable support for the innova-

---

5. Francis Walton, *Miracle of World War II* (New York: The Macmillan Company, 1956), pp. 395-397.

tive notions of men in other industries and fields of work. For instance, one can wonder if Henry Ford would have gone down in history as a great entrepreneur without the inventive activity of the administrators at A. O. Smith and many other plants.

IMPLICATIONS FOR INDIVIDUALS

Here are a few implications of this chapter for managers and would-be managers.

1. *It is wise for a manager to make it clearer to people that the order and procedure he insists on are not ends in themselves but means to ends.* Putting one new idea into practice requires discipline, restrictions, and channeling of effort.

2. *Those who consider going into management should be prepared to be rewarded both for ability in implementing ideas and for imagination in conceiving new schemes—but more often for the former.* To use a football analogy, it is more often important to carry the ball well or to help the ball carrier than to devise new plays. Lest this analogy be misunderstood, it must be understood that the manager will be under continuous pressure to carry the ball in different ways, under ever-changing conditions, against different opponents, and on different fields. The manager will occasionally even have to apply his skill to a completely different kind of game!

12

SUMMARY

AND

CONCLUSIONS

IT IS TIME NOW to summarize the qualities of the managerial mind and ask some questions about them. What do these qualities tell us about the contributions managers can and cannot make to society? What are the strengths and weaknesses of the administrative point of view?

REVIEW

In summarizing the preceding chapters, it is important to recall the definition of the manager as one who gets work done through other people. He may be a scientist managing scientists, an educator managing teachers, or a businessman managing company employees. He is *not* an executive (even with the title of manager) whose primary concern is financial manipulation, research and analysis, personal selling, or other tasks where supervision is not the crucial element. The distinction, while often a matter of emphasis and degree and not clear-cut, is vital. Furthermore, the manager may or may not be a "leader" or "entrepreneur" as those terms are often conceived. There is no reason why he cannot be both, but surely many fine managers are not great leaders, and certainly many leaders and entrepreneurs are not good administrators.

We must also remember that we have been concentrating on the *distinguishing* features but not on *all* important features. Surely analytical ability, mental quickness, good judgment, and other qualities are important to managerial success. But they are important to success in all professions. They are not what makes the managerial mind unique.

To summarize:

1. The main commitment of the managerial mind is to the organization. The administrator considers the survival, operating ability, and growth of his department, task force, or enterprise important for their own sake. He continually puts the processes of supervising and co-ordinating first in his thinking. While he finds it natural to criticize any organizational policies with which he disagrees, his opposition is loyal as long as he stays with the group. His attitude is, in effect, "My organization right or wrong, but my organization."

2. The attempt to control people for the sake of organizational objectives is, however, partly self-defeating—because the use of people as means to ends restricts their spirit and effectiveness, because power allows the manager to enforce and perpetuate his own errors, and because anxiety about these effects is a drain on his own capacity. In addition, there are chronic conflicts of interest in administration.

3. In large part, the managerial mind represents an effort to cope with these dilemmas. One of the most important answers that the administrator has come up with is to recognize, appreciate, accept, and cultivate differences in employees' ways of

thinking. Pressures for conformity may be omnipresent, as always in organizational life, but they are resisted. There are strong personal and also practical reasons for this attitude.

4. The manager also copes with the dilemmas of direction and control by placing a value on tension. He regards many forms of it as an essential ingredient of creative relationships and aggressive activity. He is interested not only in maintaining various sources of tension but also in preserving enough balance among them so that one does not overpower another.

5. The administrator is willing to disturb, probe, and look for trouble in organizational relationships. Problems and even failures are viewed as having constructive value in the struggle to survive and grow. The manager cannot eliminate the tendencies toward inertia but he can "contain" them. As a means of stimulating the aggressive spirit, he can encourage the use of quantitative measures and objective techniques in the analysis of problems; he can promote acceptance of the fact that creative relationships may be strict and hard. This approach, too, helps to cope with the chronic inefficiencies of management.

6. The man with a managerial mind is full of hesitancy to manipulate employees or intrude into their personalities. At times he may be required—by the situation or by his own inadequacies —to tell his people how to think and behave, but he is forever weighing and questioning the value of such intrusions. His preference is to manage by assigning jobs, while leaving methods and motivations up to the people performing them. This preference means, among other things, that he is willing to stand back and watch mistakes being made.

7. Realizing that set expectations frequently act as a brake on individual creativity, the administrator tries to keep them from becoming too important in his thinking. He prods employees to break old patterns of behavior and to enlarge their horizons, refuses to take seriously the limitations that people may think they have, tries to create an atmosphere that will encourage venturesomeness, and recognizes that he himself can never know

the true potentials of another man. To the extent that expectations are necessary, he considers high ones more justifiable.

8. It is also characteristic of the administrator's thinking that great importance is attached to teaching. The manager not only values teaching as a tool; he also feels that he would be virtually helpless without it. Most useful are the indirect forms of teaching —personal example, discerning questions, and the creation of guideposts for the future.

9. The manager has need of not one but three levels of knowledge—problem-solving methods, operating realities, and desirable goals and policies. The first is the most basic level; the last is generally more significant to top management than to middle and lower management. The great importance of all three levels is a distinguishing feature of the administrative mind.

10. An important test of the manager's approach is what other people are encouraged to do by his presence. They are not so afraid of making mistakes as they might otherwise be. They are more flexible, more confident of their abilities to handle whatever problems the future brings. Different groups work out their own "housekeeping" methods. A keener sense of mission and purpose runs through the organization. Managers and workers down the line feel more responsible for "running their own shows" and for the results of their decisions. Employees have a strong sense of interrelationship. The everyday conflicts of administration take on meaning and significance, and there is less *anxiety* about conflict.

11. Managerial values are creative in a variety of ways. They lead administrators to team up with inventors, to create production, marketing, financial, and other structures for new enterprises, and to infuse and nurture vitality in their organizations. What strikes some critics as a suppression of creativity often is merely the sacrifice of some good ideas urged on management in order that the organization with its limited resources may give adequate support to other projects.

These qualities have a vital bearing on questions many managers, would-be managers, and students have been asking. Is there a strong pattern of values and assumptions in the administrative outlook, as there is in a thoughtful scientist's, lawyer's, or engineer's perspective? This question is likely to be asked by the numerous technical and professional people who find themselves edging or being edged into management positions. Does the administrator *proceed to use* knowledge in predictable ways? Does he develop attitudes toward problems that are original and unusual, not likely to be found in the population at large?

It seems clear that the answers to these questions are "Yes." What is more, there can be little doubt that the managerial mind has many characteristics of the type we call "professional." Its qualities create a demand for knowledge, for disciplined thinking, for analysis, for objectivity, for communication of experience and standards. It also appears that the managerial mind, like the "legal mind" or "academic mind," for instance, is selective; that is, its requirements are not easily met by any well-meaning, intelligent person, but only by those with certain desires and dispositions.

It would be a mistake, nevertheless, to conclude that the managerial mind is exactly like other professional minds. There is more "tight-rope walking" among conflicts in the administrative point of view. Personal, physical elements are more important. Problems are messier both in definition and solution. The need for improvisation is greater. All these factors mean that the "profile" of the managerial mind is basically different. Some may interpret this argument as favorable to calling the career administrator a professional; some may interpret it in the exact opposite way.

In any case, the fact remains that the qualities of the managerial mind add up to a pattern—a strong pattern, dynamic and self-regenerating. This is the important thing. It means that the administrative point of view is second to few if any in terms

of rationale and internal logic, an idea that deserves more emphasis in the speaking and writing of practicing managers. It
means to would-be managers, students, and men "jumping the
fence" from other specialties, that the administrative mind has
much of the same appeal that other "minds" have—and more
appeal for some people.

Shortcomings and Implications

Turning now to the significance of the managerial mind for
society in general, we find that the development of this way of
thinking is not an unmixed blessing. Both debits and credits must
be taken into account. First, what are the general limitations of
the manager's point of view?

Narrowness. It has a narrowing effect. His sense of commitment to the organization tends to restrict his vision, so that,
when he turns to nonorganizational issues or fields outside administration, he may easily miss the point of what is being said
or done. He has become so habituated to putting his department,
agency, or firm first that he finds it unnatural to respond to concerns that are not at all related to organized effort. The business
manager who is suddenly put in a political office, for example,
may be as awkward as the businessman who tries to write a
novel. The whole level of his approach seems wrong to those in
the field, and he cannot understand why. I do not mean that all
managers are this way—obviously they are not. I mean only that
the managerial mind exerts a strong *influence* in this direction.

The narrowing effect of the managerial mind takes two
forms: First, the manager finds it difficult to think of regional
problems that do not involve any one organization in particular.
He makes remarks like, "What is good for General Motors is
good for the country," which may be perfectly logical in the
context of his thinking but infuriating to the many who think
their interests conflict with those of General Motors. While
progress for an organization takes place in a straight line, progress

for a region is likely to be "circular," involving efforts to move in different or even conflicting directions, which collectively create a forward movement. Franklin D. Roosevelt recognized this difference when, after many years of peacetime hostility to business leadership (which was consistent with his peacetime politics), he staffed his administration with industrial executives in order to win World War II. The war involved an organized effort to accomplish a job for the whole nation, while much of the earlier period involved political fulfillment of conflicting needs and aspirations.

Second, the manager finds it difficult to respond to some of the feelings people have in private life. Worries about love, death, anonymity, youth, insecurity, morals, and so forth are likely to "go over his head" except as he experiences them himself. He does not have the broad, trained sensitivity that a good journalist, minister, or politician must have—or that an intelligent mother has. Indeed, the demands of administration are such that his earlier sensitivity to such matters may have been progressively dulled. I wonder if it is not revealing that we are likely to find a college dean's novel treating a love affair methodically, like the consummation of a long-range plan, or a business executive in politics trying to win the voters' hearts by showing how efficient he is.

This type of narrowness is, of course, not unknown to the professional world. For instance, doctors are notorious for their obtuseness about social problems and public relations, yet no group is more dedicated to the preservation of human life.

Organization vs. community. Second, the values of the managerial mind aggravate some kinds of conflict between the organization and the community. The manager may believe in the public good with all his heart, and he may sincerely subscribe to the principle that the interests of the community should be put ahead of the interests of the organization.[1] Nevertheless, it is he

---

1. Robert W. Austin, "Code of Conduct for Executives," *Harvard Business Review*, September-October, 1961, p. 53.

who interprets the public good for the organization, and the stronger his administrative orientation, the more biased his interpretation will probably be.

For example, he may be biased by the kind of loyalty described in Chapter 1—"My organization right or wrong, but my organization." One illustration of what may happen is the decision to change to an out-of-town supplier whose prices are a little lower than those of the local supplier. The manager does not like to hurt local business, for he is aware of the implications of business failure for unemployment, inadequate taxes for schools, juvenile delinquency, and so forth; but his first loyalty is to his organization, which can meet a higher standard of performance with more efficient purchasing.

A more subtle, though perhaps more important, example is the toleration of activities that run counter to the standards of the community. I refer to the attitude described in Chapter 6— the distrust of interfering with the way an employee is doing his job as long as he produces the results management desires. This attitude may mean, as in the case of the Lincoln Electric episode, a refusal to outlaw a practice like gambling. From a community point of view, such a policy may be inexcusably lax. Ministers and teachers may protest, and the workers' families may suffer needless hardship. (The result is not always so happy as in Lincoln's case.) Another example is the northern managers of a southern plant who allow a degree of desegregation that the local people consider dangerous.

This second shortcoming of the managerial mind has implications for the system of checks and balances in a local community or the nation. Benjamin M. Selekman advocated a concept of "constitutionalism" in the structure of labor-management relations;[2] and John K. Galbraith has urged that different interests in society (producers, consumers, farmers, industrialists,

---

2. Benjamin J. Selekman, *A Moral Philosophy for Management* (New York: McGraw-Hill Book Company, Inc., 1959).

and so forth) should have equal status in mutual bargaining.[3] Both these concepts, it seems to me, gain validity because of the nature of the managerial mind. From a manager's point of view they imply compromises and concessions that he hates to make (at least, when they apply to him), but they are sound in terms of the larger social base of which organizations are a part and from which, in the long run, they draw strength and support.

Omission of many values. The managerial mind leaves out a whole set of important personal values. Values like gentleness, kindness, serenity, gracefulness, and sympathy are omitted. Managers often do value such qualities, but they necessarily emphasize the "tough," "hardboiled," analytical values and traits.

The preceding chapters offer eloquent testimony on this point. Note some of the key words and phrases. Commitment to the organization (Chapter 1) often implies a kind of *ruthlessness,* if necessary, for the sake of organizational survival. It is not by accident that the reader of many cases and documentaries in administration finds recurring statements like, "I could fire half the employees tomorrow, if I had to for the sake of the company." The acceptance of differences (Chapter 3) is also a "tough-minded" attitude, implying, as it does, living purposefully with *friction* and *disagreement.* With the attitude toward tension (Chapter 4) we have associated such key words as *conflict* and *resistance.* Zest for problems (Chapter 5) implies *upsetting comfortable routines, disturbing people,* and *pushing* to do better. In connection with distrust of manipulation (Chapter 6), we noted that it often means more *demanding,* more *challenging* standards. As for expectations (Chapter 7), the administrator is practically *never satisfied* that he or others have done the best that he or they can do. In the section on teaching (Chapter 8), it appears that some of the most effective methods revolve around *probing questions* and the *self-searching* required

---

3. John K. Galbraith, *American Capitalism, The Concept of Countervailing Power* (Boston: Houghton Mifflin Company, 1952).

in planning. As for the effects of the administrator's thinking on people, the key words range from *venturesomeness* and *self-reliance* to *performance*. The emphasis is on what people can do, an emphasis that implicitly favors the strong, the shrewd, the "result-getters."

The moral, it seems to me, is that the managerial mind has a kind of built-in myopia that should be recognized and allowed for. The gentle values—managers may describe them as "soft" values—are no less important because they are left out of the administrative creed. We must keep the manager's example in perspective, using his life as but one source of guidance, instruction, and inspiration—and remembering that when he is successful it is only because predecessors have built a basis for co-operative living by teaching the kinder values.

Toll on health. Managerial attitudes are hard on the health and emotions. The difference in the amount of stress encountered in business by the manager and the accountant may be even greater than that in medicine between the general practitioner and the dermatologist (the incidence of heart attacks among the latter, who operate under less stress, reportedly is only one-third that of the former) or that in law between the trial lawyer and the legal researcher.

This heavy toll on mind and body can be attributed to a variety of causes. An obvious one is the situation alluded to in Chapter 2. The tendency of management to work against itself and the constant conflicts of interest in a successful administrative career doubtless add large doses of anxiety in many a supervisor's life. Another cause is the unpopularity that often attends management. In tolerating a reasonably high amount of tension, in willingness to disturb routines and press for new solutions, in insistence on high standards of performance, the administrator is not unlikely to "go against the grain" of many employees and lose an element of popular support that he might otherwise enjoy. The administrator is also under pressure to subordinate his personal needs and desires to the demands of his professional life, which may also "take something out of him." Much the same thing happens when the attorney recognizes that "the law is a jealous mistress" or when the doctor "marries medicine." In the words of a college president writing about the executive life:

"The good of the company" often comes ahead of his personal pleasures or convenience. He must be the life of the party, whether he feels like it or not. If his fatigue, indigestion, boredom, or even disagreement on moral questions become too evident to his friends, there is something wrong with the company, or he must be a bad choice for the office. The test is a hard one. Any Dr. Jekyll, when he is honest, will want to be a Mr. Hyde at least once a month. . . . [4]

The implications of these drains on health? For one, young men considering management as a career should consider carefully whether or not they are "built" right for the administrative side of the organization. Not all of us have Churchill's stomach. Some of our most promising young minds may, I suspect, do far better as specialists in organizations than as "general practitioners."

Another implication is procedural. The stress and distress of operations is an argument for checks and balances on decision-makers. Going from crisis to crisis, never satisfied, often living irregular hours, and sometimes losing their perspectives as a result, these men may keenly resent any compromises of their authority even though they may profit from them in the end. Are there easily negotiable channels of communication so that a subordinate can go over his boss's head to an executive higher up when unreasonableness or unfairness are being carried too far? Are there provisions for "audits" of organizational problems and thinking by independent outsiders who may say what an executive's subordinates fear to say about his policies? Should more use be made of the committee system to "check out" proposed decisions before they go into effect? Surely there are argu-

---

4. Louis W. Norris, "Moral Hazards of an Executive," *Harvard Business Review*, September-October, 1960, p. 78.

ments on both sides of each such question, and the health factor is not decisive. In each case, however, it provides a further argument for the checks.

Still another implication involves arrangements for maintaining health. In Brooklyn, the Grace Medical Group has attracted attention for its service to various banks and companies in the New York area. Grace offers the advantages of a well-rounded group of specialists and generalists under one roof, who try to maintain friendly, helpful, informal relationships with employees in client organizations. Another approach is the in-company medical department, and certainly great strides have been made in improving both the concept and technical proficiency of such groups. Equally noteworthy is the kind of comprehensive health care and insurance program instituted at Harvard University several years ago and now under consideration at other colleges and universities.

Demands for knowledge. This last item is less a restriction than a challenge and a possible danger. Leading administrators make implicit promises to employees and the public that are not easy to fill. They imply that, given proper opportunity, their management groups will produce strong, useful organizations and harness individual potentials. Now, particularly in business, this claim is noteworthy. The Robber Barons of another era made no such claim, nor do today's "wheelers and dealers." The latter are committed to the search for personal riches. They may rationalize their personal rewards as beneficial to others, but any such benefits are a by-product rather than the main purpose of their activities. By contrast, the William Givens, Ralph Cordiners, and Frederick Kappels imply that, "These ideas about organizational effectiveness and self-fulfillment are vitally important to us. Give us the chance and we will make them work."

Achieving such purposes requires more than hard work, dedication, and the kinds of attitudes described in previous chapters, however. It calls for a good deal of sophisticated knowledge of resources and human behavior that the manager by himself cannot develop. For example, what is the optimum of tension in a government office (see Chapter 4)? Unless the manager knows, he may make some serious mistakes. In a scientific organization, what are the predictable effects of mixing different kinds of people (see Chapter 3) in various ways? One combination may be far more productive than another. In a highly competitive consumer-goods industry, what corporate financial policies will help most to assure long-term growth and strength? Survival itself may depend on the answer. In an educational organization, what kinds of control data will accurately mirror the performance of different functions and departments, some semi-autonomous and some not? Without good appraisals, it is hard to know what to ask from the members.

Private companies, researchers, foundations, associations, universities, and other agencies have been making impressive efforts indeed to acquire answers to a long series of such questions. But while they have been working, the demands on organizations have been rising, too—not simply because of the promises of managers but also because of workers' growing dependence on organizations and because of the increasingly pervasive effects of organizations on society. Will enough new knowledge be made available in useful form in time to meet rising needs? If not, will managers be able to cope with the reaction? The challenge is not unlike that which lawyers might face if justice began to miscarry often in the courts, for the legal mind implicitly promises justice. Fortunately for the law, a tremendous body of case information has long since been developed and disseminated to guide judges, attorneys, and clients.

CONTRIBUTIONS

Having considered the "costs" and shortcomings of the managerial mind, let us turn now to the other side of the question. What does this way of thinking contribute to society? What positive gains does it produce?

First, the organization gains stature as a result of the administrator's commitments to it, and this gain is significant because the organization has become a vehicle not only of progress but of survival. Without strong organizations, a nation cannot have a strong defense; meet the demands of feeding, clothing, and housing a burgeoning population; educate a teeming school population to live in a fast-changing world; or perform countless other vital functions.

Second, the administrator's approach helps people to develop their capacities to work in association with each other. For example, as already indicated, the values placed on individual differences and tension help to break down the notion that working relationships should be full of "sweetness and light." These values also help employees to make use of one another instead of forming rigid relationships. Gains of this type are reinforced by the zest for problems: employees are encouraged to take the attitude that "the real problems are our own problems, and there is practically nothing we can't do if we can work well enough together."

This type of development is meaningful because the problems of co-operative work consume a large portion of people's thinking, even in a so-called leisure society. Freed of false inhibitions against tension, differences of opinion, problems, and so forth, employees waste less time in futile worry. They find it natural to take an active, aggressive interest in what goes on in the organization; they shun the role of passive spectators and find release in participation. To the extent that the need for excitement and participation at work affects a people's psychology, therefore, the national character takes on more tone, more resilience.

Third, the administrative approach helps to satisfy the desire for achievement. The achievement motive runs high in modern culture,[5] and its consummation or frustration seems to have profound implications for society.

---

5. David McClelland, *The Achieving Society* (Princeton: Van Nostrand, 1961).

The manager's contribution in this respect is twofold. For one thing, there are many goals a person cannot achieve alone, and the manager seeks to improve the mechanics of achievement by making the organization a more fertile place to work. The question is whether it is to be a "chamber of horrors" or a constructive outlet for energy and aspiration. Equally important, the administrator aims to stimulate employees to set higher goals than they otherwise would—and even to create goals they would not otherwise formulate. It is interesting to see how people's expectations of themselves and others tend to rise when they confront mutual problems and accept the friction and striving that go with solving them. We often hear it said that groups compromise goals, and no doubt that does happen from time to time, especially when there is no sense of purpose among members. It is far more common, however, in my observation, for men to raise their sights when they work together—not only because the common fund of information is increased, but also because there is usually a subtle prodding going on in the discussions and interchanges.

Fourth, the attitudes of the managerial mind make administration a happier task. The man with these attitudes does not suffer (as we are told so many people today do) from a lack of involvement in absorbing causes; he is highly involved.

Equally important, he has no false images of what managerial life should be like. Disagreements, problems, striving, falling short are inevitable and are not considered black marks. They are regarded as natural and, to a point, valuable. The manager is not ambivalent in this respect. He does not feel a compulsion to hold up serenity and harmony as ideals at the same time that, in his personal actions, he works for different values. He does not feel that he and his organization must always be "successful." He does not feel constrained to create an image of a conservative, a defender of the status quo, when in reality he is a radical working always for change. He does not feel, if he is a manager in business, that he must act as if profits were his only goal when in fact the growth of the organization for its own sake consumes much of his time.

In addition, there are the prospects of young men and women thinking of going into management. They are often led into unhappy careers, it seems to me, by fuzzy images of what the executive is trying to do. The executive who is a "wheeler and dealer" is one type; the executive who acts as a sort of moderator in a democratic process is another; the executive who accomplishes his goals mainly by himself (the economic analyst, for example) is a third type; the executive who gets things done through people—whom I call the manager or administrator—is still another type.

Each of these executives leads a life quite different from those of the other three, both in the satisfactions he obtains and in the effects he sustains. The young man who goes into business looking for money and who falls instead into work calling for strong administrative ideals; the young person whose personal inclinations are toward the scholarly, analytical approach and who instead ends up with the reins to a team of men pulling in different directions; the student with a strong aptitude for personal supervisory leadership who heads unwittingly into a string of positions calling for mediation and conciliation—these men are inviting frustration, bitterness, and disillusionment in their lives. If they could distinguish or if counselors could distinguish for them between the values emphasized by the administrator and the values emphasized by others who are executives but not administrators, their chances for happiness and self-fulfillment would be greater.

Fifth—and closely related—a clearer understanding of the administrator's way of thinking should help to dispel the apologetic feelings described in the Introduction. This advantage, too, strengthens the prospects of self-fulfillment in management work.

Finally, an appreciation of the managerial mind tells us something about how to achieve a "balanced" society. I refer to the fast-growing and dangerous imbalance that overshadows the current scene in the United States and other affluent nations.

As described by Benjamin M. Selekman, for instance, there has been tremendous growth in science and technology and in the corporation and government, but man's social institutions have not grown nearly so fast and in some cases have even retrogressed. In medicine, social work, education, art, music, and similar areas we are "woefully behind." The situation is laden with explosive consequences, feeding tendencies to hostility, aggression, and self-destructive behavior.[6]

Two points must be emphasized: First, our social institutions are not likely to catch up unless mobilized by strong organizations. It is significant, I think, that the full-time professional administrator is already beginning to find his way into the field. In a small but growing number of hospitals, adult-education agencies, youth-service centers, and other such organizations he is taking his place beside the doctor, professor, or other specialist. Second, the administrative attitudes that have arisen in business, government, the military, and public schools and universities are not peculiar to those institutions alone. They are equally appropriate in other situations where work much be accomplished through organization. The sense of commitment to the organization, the acceptance of differences, the value placed on tension—these and other thought patterns already described ought to have as much validity in a medical group, civic symphony enterprise, or Y.M.C.A. as they have in a steel company or antitrust department.

Our social institutions may therefore be well able to take advantage of the transferability of values and skills. They can profit from the knowledge that the administrative point of view is an intense, absorbing, demanding one, not quickly acquired by the beginner nor easily applied on a "week-end volunteer" basis by the most seasoned manager.

As for the administrator himself, I suspect that in many respects his future is about the same in any organization, in any place.

---

6. Benjamin M. Selekman, "Businessmen in Power," *Harvard Business Review*, September-October, 1961, p. 95.

His efforts can never be completely successful; the dilemmas of management and control will always be with him. He has the gift of being able to be absorbed in his work, however, to immerse himself in turning suffering into growth, argument into creativity, defeat into progress. People may say that he "seems to take a beating," but he does not resist the daily give and take. He belongs to it, and it to him. His regret, if he has any, is not that his commitments make life so strenuous, but that he does not have more capacity to become involved and more sensitivity to all of the implications of his approach.

INDEX

INDEX